Understanding Industrial Practices in
Food Technology

ELLIE HALLAM

Series editor
LESLEY CRESSWELL

Text © Ellie Hallam, Lesley Cresswell 2005
Original illustrations © Nelson Thornes Ltd 2005

The right of Ellie Hallam and Lesley Cresswell to be identified as authors of this work has been asserted by them in accordance with the Copyright, Designs and Patents Act 1988.

All rights reserved. The copyright holders authorise ONLY users of *Understanding Industrial Practices in Food Technology* to make photocopies of the glossary and worksheets for their own or their students' immediate use within the teaching context. No other rights are granted without permission in writing from the publishers or under licence from the Copyright Licensing Agency Limited. Further details of such licences (for reprographic reproduction) may be obtained from the Copyright Licensing Agency Limited, of 90 Tottenham Court Road, London W1T 4LP.

Copy by any other means or for any other purpose is strictly prohibited without prior written consent from the copyright holders. Application for such permission should be addressed to the publishers.

Any person who commits any unauthorised act in relation to this publication may be liable to criminal prosecution and civil claims for damages.

Published in 2005 by:
Nelson Thornes Ltd
Delta Place
27 Bath Road
CHELTENHAM
GL53 7TH
United Kingdom

06 07 08 09 / 10 9 8 7 6 5 4 3 2

A catalogue record for this book is available from the British Library

ISBN 0 7487 9020 9

Edited by Judi Hunter
Illustrations by Peters and Zabransky
Page make-up by Northern Phototypesetting Co Ltd, Bolton

Printed and bound in Croatia by Zrinski

Acknowledgements
The publishers are grateful to the following for permission to reproduce photographs and other copyright material:
Cover photographs: Corel 227 (top); Digital Stock 7 (middle); Stockbyte 31 (bottom)

Based on an image provided by NutriCalc (p10); Stuart Sweatmore (p57)

Every effort has been made to contact copyright holders. The publishers apologise to anyone whose rights have been inadvertently overlooked, and will be happy to rectify any errors or omissions.

Introduction

Understanding Industrial Practices in Food Technology covers the key terms relating to industrial designing and manufacturing. It aims to support students undertaking GCSE Technology and GCSE Manufacturing (Double Award) courses. The book will help students and teachers understand what industrial practice is, what Systems and Control means and how to integrate these aspects into coursework using simple industry-related activities. For exam revision the book will be invaluable in helping students gain a good grasp of terminology and theory, both essential for exam success.

The first part of the book is set out in an A–Z format. Each photocopiable entry begins with a clear definition of the term, followed by an explanation and examples. Throughout the text there are frequent references to coursework requirements. This ensures students know what they have to do and why. These are followed by Coursework checkpoints which show the direct application of the term to students' own coursework.

The second part of the book provides photocopiable worksheets that are associated with the key A–Z terms. The worksheets and A–Z definitions can be used as teaching resources and support individual students in their own coursework.

What are industrial practices?

At KS4 the curriculum follows a design and manufacturing process that is based on an industrial model. In industry these designing and manufacturing processes enable manufacturers to make cost-effective products at a profit. At KS4 these activities are referred to as 'industrial practices'.

Many industrial practices make use of CAD/CAM and Information and Communication Technology (ICT). These have revolutionised the way industry works, enabling companies to communicate information quickly and to design and manufacture on a global scale. Developing this capability in schools has required access to specialist computer software and ICT links, to enhance designing, modelling, communicating, manufacturing and control.

Why do we need to include industrial practices in Technology and Manufacturing?

An understanding of industrial practices is part of the requirements of the KS4 curriculum for Design and Technology and Manufacturing. They are also practices used by industry to achieve the successful manufacture of innovative products that provide valuable exports. Industrial practices used in this way enable and encourage creativity.

We need to use industrial practices in the same way, as *processes* that enable students to design and make innovative products. We also need to provide a curriculum that is relevant and forward looking. Using up-to-date industrial practices will enable us to do this. Bringing manufacturing into the classroom will give students:

- a wider understanding of industry and what it has to offer
- an understanding of how ICT has revolutionised industry, enabling manufacturing on a global scale
- the opportunity for improved motivation and higher levels of achievement.

Introduction

How to use this book

The book addresses students directly in order to encourage independent learning. This means that many of the Coursework checkpoints and worksheet activities can be used for homework, or as focused practical tasks.

The A–Z terms (pp. 1–88) are carefully cross-referenced with some terms appearing in a different typeface. This means that more information about that term can be found on another page. Students can look up the meaning of key industrial terms and use the definitions for exam revision. Following the A–Z section, the Key people involved in the production process are identified (p. 89), and their roles clearly defined.

The references to coursework requirements will help students understand why they need to include industrial practices in their own coursework. They can then use the Coursework checkpoint activities to help them undertake activities related to their own coursework. Coursework checklists (p. 90) include tips on planning and producing their work, and are followed by Key words (p. 91) to encourage students to use industrial terms in the context of their own work.

The ready-to-use worksheets (pp. 92–140) are also cross-referenced. Terms that are listed in the A–Z section appear in a different typeface. This provides a reference for the A–Z sheets that will need to be copied to support the worksheet activities.

a

accelerated freeze drying (AFD) is a process used to preserve foods such as instant coffee and vegetables that are to be used in soup mixes.

- The vegetables are cut up into small pieces, frozen and then transferred to a freeze drier. Here, they are placed in a strong vacuum and heated slightly.
- Under vacuum, water boils well below 100°C (its boiling point at normal pressure) and so the water in the vegetables sublimes (is converted directly from ice into water vapour).
- The vapour can then be carried away, leaving the vegetable pieces dry.

Freeze dried foods are expensive to produce but they are high quality as they rehydrate very easily when used.

acidity regulators are additives that are used in some foods to make sure that the level of acidity in the food is the same every time it is made. They are used mainly in fruit-based foods such as jam, some fruit drinks, fruit pies and mince pies. Fruits are natural products and so the level of acidity present in them may vary, depending on when the fruit is harvested, or what the weather has been like while the fruit has been growing.

acids are used in food manufacture for a number of reasons.

- Lemon juice, which contains citric acid, can be added to yoghurt to provide 'sharpness' to taste.
- Vinegar (ethanoic or acetic acid) is used in pickles and mincemeat and lactic acid is used in processed cheese to help preserve the food. These acids also add to the taste, which is a secondary function of the acid. Vinegar may also be used in bread to prevent it from going mouldy in hot weather.
- Citric acid (in lemon juice) is often added to fruit salads to prevent browning.
- Acids can alter the texture of a starch gel, or an egg-white foam. For example, citric acid will make a starch gel softer. Vinegar or cream of tartar will make egg-white foam more stable.
- Cream of tartar or acid calcium phosphate is used as a component of baking powder. This is a chemical raising agent used in cake making. The acid reacts with sodium hydrogen carbonate to produce carbon dioxide.
- Ascorbic acid (vitamin C) is used as an antioxidant in some fruit drinks and cereal bars. It is also used to treat flour that is used for bread making.

additives are chemicals that are added to foods in small amounts to enhance the food. The use of food additives is controlled by law and many have been given E numbers. Additives are divided into a number of different categories. These include:

- acidity regulators
- anti-caking agents
- antioxidants
- artificial sweeteners

In your coursework project you will need to:

- understand that additives can be used for specific purposes in food manufacture.

Understanding Industrial Practices: Food Technology © Nelson Thornes 2005

- colours
- emulsifiers
- flavour enhancers and flavourings
- gelling agents
- preservatives
- raising agents
- stabilisers and thickeners.

> **Coursework checkpoint:** *additives*
>
> Check out examples of foods that contain additives.
>
> 1. Examine the **ingredients lists** on foods in your cupboard and fridge at home.
> 2. Make a list showing the name of the food, the category of additive and the name of the additive used.
> 3. Explain the function of the additives used in each food.

In your coursework project you will need to:

- use different methods for creating aeration in food products
- assess the effects of each method upon the volume, texture and **flavour** of the product.

aeration is the trapping of air in a food. It increases the volume of the food and alters its texture, making the food lighter and more pleasant to eat. Air can be introduced into the food by beating, using yeast or chemicals. For example:

- egg-whites are beaten to form a foam when making meringues and a batter mixture is beaten when making Yorkshire puddings.
- yeasts are a type of **micro-organism** that are used in bread making. The yeast produces gas by **fermentation**. The gas is trapped in the dough by the gluten in the flour and so the bread rises.
- chemical **raising agents** such as sodium hydrogen carbonate react with acids to produce gas. This reaction occurs when using self-raising flour and baking powder for making cakes.

In your coursework project you will need to:

- understand that **finishing processes** can be used to improve the aesthetic properties of food products
- use **computer-aided design (CAD)** to design packaging that enhances the aesthetic appeal of your product.

aesthetic properties relate to the appearance, colour, texture and taste of a product. These properties must match the expectations of the purchaser. Most foods are sold already packaged with the food itself not visible, so the appearance of the packaging is important. The food itself must also be aesthetically appealing, so that **consumers** are happy to keep buying the product.

ambient temperature is the temperature of the surroundings: it can be taken to be room temperature. Bacteria that can spoil foods or cause food-poisoning (**pathogens**) will grow and multiply at typical room temperatures. Foods that are designed to be stored under ambient conditions must be processed in a way that will prevent micro-organisms (bacteria, yeast and moulds) from growing. This is achieved using preservation methods.

anti-caking agents are additives that are added to dry, powdered foods such as salt and icing sugar. They absorb any moisture from the atmosphere without becoming wet themselves, so that the product remains free-flowing.

antioxidants are additives that are used in foods to prevent **fat** from becoming rancid. This is characterised by an unpleasant smell and flavour. Rancidity develops through an oxidation reaction that takes place when air comes into contact with the fat. Light and some metals can speed up the rate of reaction, so fatty foods are usually packed in light-proof packaging. Metal **packaging materials** are kept out of contact with the food. Ascorbic acid is an example of an antioxidant that is found in some fruit drinks and in cereal bars.

the **appearance** of food is important in making it attractive to consumers. A **design brief** for a new product will give a description of what the finished product is expected to look like. Factors such as size, shape and **colour** are described as part of the product appearance. Finishing **processes**, such as glazing, garnishing, icing, piping or dusting with sugar can be used to enhance appearance. Food appearance is also an important **quality indicator** and will be checked as part of **quality control (QC)** procedures.

> **Coursework checkpoint:** *appearance*
> ○ Write a description of the appearance of a pizza with cheese and tomato topping that could be used for quality control **testing**.
> ○ State the size of the pizza (the diameter of its base for a round pizza) and include enough detail about its topping so that anyone making the pizza would know if it was satisfactory and met the quality control requirement.

artificial sweeteners are **additives** that are used to replace sucrose (table sugar) in products that are suitable for diabetics and in those that are designed to appeal to slimmers. They provide sweetness without the calories that sucrose (a **carbohydrate**) would provide. Saccharin, acesulfame K and aspartame are among approved sweeteners that have been given **E numbers**.

aroma is the attractive smell given off by a food, often as it is being cooked. It is caused by volatile compounds (those that boil at temperatures well below 100°C) evaporating as the food is heated. Spices and herbs, for example, can be used to enhance aroma and increase the attractiveness of a food.

assembly line is an alternative name for the production line.

automation enables the operation and control of production processes using electronic or computer **control systems**, such as programmable logic controllers (PLCs). Once automatic machines are set up, they repeat processes continuously without the need for further human control (unless something goes wrong).

Most automated systems make use of sensors to monitor and control the machines. Sensors provide **feedback** to the system so that changes are made to the process when necessary. For example, filled cans of soup will be weighed automatically before they are sterilised. If they do not contain enough soup they will be too light and they will be automatically rejected from the **production line**. At the same time, a feedback loop will increase the amount of soup being deposited into the cans. Sensors can also detect faults or shut down a machine if there is a potential danger to the operator, the machine or the product.

In the food industry, many processing operations take place at very high speed and automated production using **computer-aided manufacture (CAM)** is essential if the factory is to reach its production targets. Automation enables fast and accurate repeat manufacture and the production of cost-effective reliable products.

In your coursework project you will need to:

- consider the appearance of the product you are developing and measure its appeal to consumers in your **target market group**
- use finishing processes where necessary to enhance the appearance of your product
- include a description of the appearance of your product in your **product specification**.

bacteria are a type of micro-organism. They can grow and multiply very quickly if conditions are suitable. Usually they multiply by cells dividing into two, but some bacteria can also form spores. Spores are more difficult to destroy than the dividing cells and food preservation processes must take this into account.

There are many types of bacteria. Some are used to produce food products such as yoghurt, through **fermentation**.

- Some bacteria such as Salmonella, Listeria and E. coli can cause food-poisoning. Bacteria that cause disease and food-poisoning are called **pathogens**. Food **manufacturers** must make sure that the processes they use destroy all pathogens within the food, so that **food safety** is assured.

- Other types of bacteria can cause food to spoil. For example, bacteria can cause milk to go sour if it is kept for too long or if it is left out of the fridge on a hot day. Food must be treated or stored in such a way that these spoilage bacteria cannot multiply quickly and cause problems during the **shelf life** of the food. If milk is pasteurised before it reaches the **consumer**, all the pathogens and many spoilage bacteria are destroyed. If the milk is kept chilled and used within a few days it will not spoil. If the milk is kept too long, or allowed to get warm, then the surviving spoilage bacteria will grow, multiply and spoil the milk.

Bacteria are living organisms. In order to grow and multiply they need:

- food (nutrients)
- water
- a suitable temperature
- a suitable pH (level of acidity)
- the correct atmosphere. (Most bacteria need oxygen, but some can only grow when oxygen is absent. A few can grow whether oxygen is present or not.)

Food preservation methods must make sure that one or more of these needs is absent from the food, so that bacteria cannot grow and multiply.

In your coursework project you will need to:

- design a food product that could be manufactured in quantity
- choose the most suitable **method of production** for your food product and give reasons for choosing it
- understand what is meant by batch production, why it is used for manufacturing products and how it compares with other methods of production

---

batch production is used when only a limited amount of the food product is required. A batch is the finished product that is made during a single production run. This may be what is made from one mix of the product or several mixes may be made. These mixes are packaged immediately, one after the other, to form a batch of product. Batch production is used for products with a short **shelf life** because they must be delivered immediately to the shops. It is also used for all products other than those where there is a demand for **high volume production** or where products are **custom made**.

Wherever possible, **manufacturers** use **production planning** to ensure that similar products are made one after the other, on one **production line**. This minimises the time lost in changing over from making one product to the next.

The use of **Information and Communication Technology (ICT)** enables the retailer's **Electronic Point of Sale (EPOS)** tills to collect and send product sales information via electronic links to the manufacturer, to allow quick response to changes in demand. Products can then be delivered from stock or made to order in a very short time. Batch production used in this way reduces the amount of stock that retailers need to keep, which saves space and cuts costs.

- understand that using **standard components** can make manufacturing more cost-effective
- understand how **quality assurance** systems and **quality control** techniques are used to manufacture high **quality** products.

binding is the technique used to make loose food ingredients stick together.

- **Egg** can be used as a binding ingredient, for example in Quorn™ or pasta. It also enhances the nutritional value of the food.
- Water can be used as a binder with **flour** in **pastry** or pasta, with rusk in burgers and sausages or with potato in croquettes or fishcakes.

biological value refers to the nutritional quality of **proteins**.

- Generally, animal products such as meat have a high biological value.
- Cereal products, such as bread, cakes and cornflakes have a lower biological value.

By mixing foods from different sources the biological value of the protein in a meal can be raised. Pulses (such as beans and peas) can be mixed with cereal foods. For example, the protein in beans on toast will have a higher biological value than if either bread or baked beans are eaten on their own.

biotechnology involves the use of **micro-organisms** or **enzymes** in food production.

- In yoghurt production, for example, **bacteria** ferment the **sugar** in milk.
- In cheese production, bacteria, moulds and **enzymes** all play a part in the production of different types of cheese.
- Quorn™ is an example of a new food that has been produced using biotechnology. It is a high protein food that can be used to replace meat in the diet.
- Biotechnology is also used to produce **genetically modified (GM)** seeds that can be used for food production.

blanching is a mild heat treatment carried out between 90–100°C. It is used to make sure that the **enzymes** in fruits and vegetables can no longer take part in chemical reactions. Blanching is a rapid process, taking 1–5 minutes, depending on the size and structure of the food. For example, slices of apple or cauliflower florets will blanch more quickly than diced carrot or swede. Blanching also destroys some **micro-organisms**.

a **brand** is the name given to a product that is marketed under the company's chosen brand name or trade mark. The brand name protects and promotes the product, so that it can't be copied legitimately by any other **manufacturer**.

Historically, branding has been used at:
- trade level for raw ingredients
- **consumer** level for retail products, e.g. 'Coca cola' and 'Cadbury' are brand names that are promoted worldwide.

FOODZ 4 U

It can be fun to decide on a suitable brand name and design a brand logo when you are developing a product of your own

Manufacturers want to build up a strong brand name that encourages brand loyalty so that consumers are willing to try new products in the range. Brand loyalty also helps to protect the manufacturer's market share of sales as customers are less likely to try similar products by other manufacturers.

browning of some fruits and vegetables occurs when they are peeled or the skin is broken in some way so that the cells in the flesh are damaged. This reaction involves enzymes in the fruit or vegetable. Apples sometimes go brown in this way while they are being eaten. Manufacturers need to prevent browning from occurring. This is done by blanching or by treating the food with lemon juice or ascorbic acid (vitamin C). The browning reaction can be slowed by placing the food in a refrigerator or by covering it with water. These methods may be used in the home or in catering.

bulk delivery of ingredients is often used by large-scale manufacturers. Flour, starch, sugar, yeast and vegetable oil can all be delivered in bulk tankers. This method saves time and money compared with the same ingredients being delivered in bags. It is also environmentally friendly as no bags have to be disposed of.

a **buying specification** (ingredient specification) is written out for every ingredient that the manufacturer buys from their suppliers. The specification gives details about the characteristics and the quality indicators of the ingredients to be supplied. For example:

- A fish finger manufacturer might write that the fish blocks supplied must be 100% cod. If they are found to contain a percentage of other fish and the manufacturer uses them to make 'cod fish fingers' they could be liable for prosecution.
- A dried soup mix manufacturer might write that dried carrot pieces must be a certain size. If they are too large they will not rehydrate quickly enough when the consumer makes the soup. If they are too small, they will look unattractive.

C

canning is a widely used method of food preservation that has been in use for well over 100 years. A weighed amount of food is placed in the can, which is sealed. The food then undergoes heat processing. The processing time and temperature must be very closely controlled to make sure that *all* the food in the can receives sufficient heat. This ensures that any bacteria and their spores inside the can are killed.

Canned foods have a very long shelf life, as long as the can is not damaged in any way. Canned foods can be stored at ambient temperature, which means there is no additional cost for storing them as there is for chilled or frozen foods.

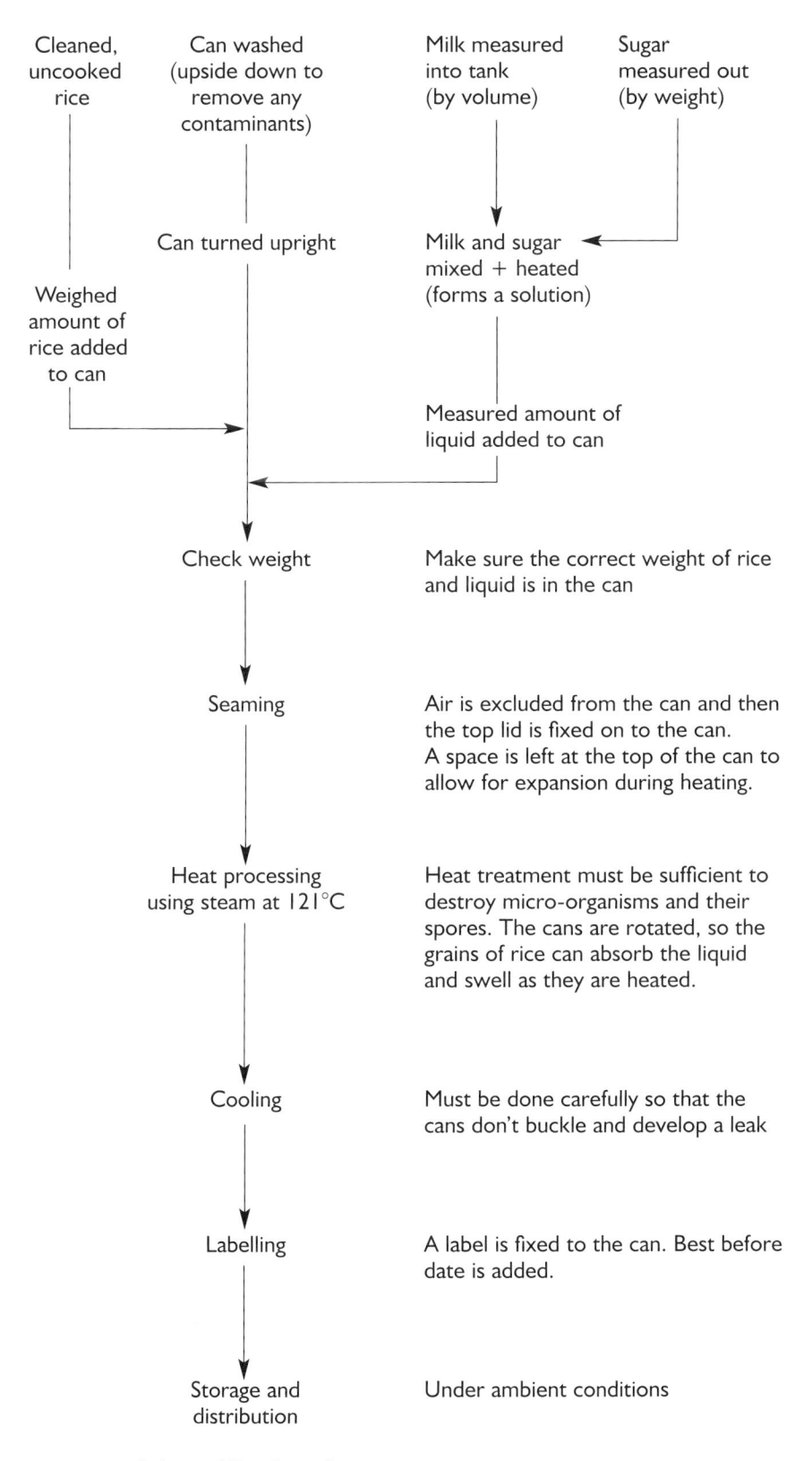

```
Cleaned,         Can washed          Milk measured      Sugar
uncooked         (upside down to     into tank          measured out
rice             remove any          (by volume)        (by weight)
                 contaminants)
   │                  │                    │                │
   │                  │                    ▼                │
   │           Can turned upright    Milk and sugar ◄───────┘
   │                  │              mixed + heated
   │                  │              (forms a solution)
Weighed               │                    │
amount of             │                    │
rice added            │                    ▼
to can                │              Measured amount of
   │                  │              liquid added to can
   └──────────────►   ◄────────────────────┘
                      ▼
                Check weight          Make sure the correct weight of rice
                      │               and liquid is in the can
                      ▼
                   Seaming            Air is excluded from the can and then
                      │               the top lid is fixed on to the can.
                      │               A space is left at the top of the can to
                      │               allow for expansion during heating.
                      ▼
               Heat processing        Heat treatment must be sufficient to
               using steam at 121°C   destroy micro-organisms and their
                      │               spores. The cans are rotated, so the
                      │               grains of rice can absorb the liquid
                      │               and swell as they are heated.
                      ▼
                   Cooling            Must be done carefully so that the
                      │               cans don't buckle and develop a leak
                      ▼
                  Labelling           A label is fixed to the can. Best before
                      │               date is added.
                      ▼
                Storage and           Under ambient conditions
                distribution
```

How canned rice pudding is made

carbohydrates such as **sugars**, pectin and **starch** have a number of **functional properties** that make them important food ingredients. All these substances can easily be digested and provide energy for the **consumer**. A few carbohydrates cannot be digested by humans and these form the dietary fibre which is essential for the maintenance of good health. These carbohydrates are referred to as **non-starch polysaccharides (NSPs)**.

chemical processing is used to describe a production operation that causes chemical changes in food. Most foods undergo some chemical changes when they are processed, especially during **heat processing**, including cooking and baking. Foods that have been chemically changed cannot then be separated into their original ingredients.

chilling involves the removal of heat from food so that its temperature is lowered to below 5°C. In industry, chilling is carried out in blast chillers that work in exactly the same way as blast freezers, but at temperatures between −1°C−+4°C. Chilling is used to extend the **shelf life** of foods for a limited period. It is often used to support another preservation method, for example, milk that has been pasteurised is kept in a refrigerator.

- Chilling does not kill any **bacteria**, but many find it too cold to grow and some will grow only slowly. The food will not spoil as fast as it would at **ambient temperature**, but it will still only keep for a limited period.
- It is important to be sure that the chiller temperature is low enough at all times. If the temperature rises, bacteria might grow in the food. These bacteria cannot be seen, but the food might become unsafe to eat. Chiller temperature is a **critical control point (CCP)** for food **manufacturers** and retailers. The chiller temperature will be controlled by computer, with an alarm that will sound if the temperature rises above a pre-set point. A **quality control (QC)** technician will check the chiller temperature at regular intervals and keep a record of the reading. In this way, the company *knows* that food is being kept at the correct temperature. If the chiller starts to go wrong, any changes in the temperature pattern will be detected by regularly examining the technician's records.
- The temperature in the home fridge should also be checked regularly. In warm weather the thermostat should be reset to make sure the food is kept cold enough.

> **Coursework checkpoint 1:** *chilling*
>
> Some foods have the words 'once opened, keep refrigerated' written on their container. These foods have been packaged in such a way that there are no **micro-organisms** within the packs. However, once the pack is opened, bacteria, yeast or moulds may reach the food and start to grow. Putting the food into the fridge will slow the rate at which this happens.
>
> ○ Make sure that you include the correct storage instructions on the packaging for your own food product.
>
> ○ Include in your coursework folder brief notes about the need to keep chilled food products at the correct temperature.

> **Coursework checkpoint 2:** *chilling*
>
> To prevent the growth of bacteria in foods the temperature in a refrigerator should be below 5°C. Check the temperature of your fridge at home to make sure it is cold enough. Do this each day for a week or two and draw a graph showing how the temperature varies with time. If your home fridge temperature is too high then ask if you can adjust the temperature control setting. Continue to monitor the temperature until you are sure that it is below 5°C.

cleaning is needed for primary food materials coming into the food factory. Field crops may contain soil, stones, weed seeds, pieces of stalk and leaves, etc. These impurities must be removed before the food is processed. Several different techniques are used for cleaning, depending upon the food material and the type of impurity.

- Sieving can be used to remove impurities if they are a different size to the food.
- Stones may be the same size as the food and they can be removed from vegetables by wet-cleaning. The vegetables pass along a trough of water and stones sink to the bottom.
- Wheat must be dry-cleaned, so a different method must be used. The wheat is lifted on a current of air. The stones are heavier so they are not lifted and can then be moved away.

the **cold chain** is the name given to the series of stages that a frozen food passes through once it is frozen, until it reaches the consumer's freezer.

colour is an important factor in the appearance of food as it gives it eye-appeal and makes us want to eat it. Food manufacturers have to ensure that the colour of the food they produce is attractive. For example, fruits and vegetables of different colours might be used in a sauce or a prepared fruit salad to give eye-appeal. Colour is also added to foods such as sweets to make them look attractive.

- Colour is also associated with flavour. For example, we expect strawberry flavoured foods to be pink-red and lemon flavoured foods to be yellow. For this reason, a raspberry flavoured jelly may have a red colour added to it.
- The natural colour associated with food is often affected during processing. For example, chlorophyll that is responsible for the green colour in vegetables will become an unattractive olive green when vegetables are heat processed during canning. Colour is often added to the product to compensate for this. Adding colour means that the food product can be made to look the same every time it is made.
- Colours that are added to foods may be either synthetic or natural. For example, banana flavoured foods may have yellow colours such as curcumin (an artificial colour) or beta-carotene (a natural colour) added to them. No colour may be used until it has undergone rigorous testing to ensure that it is safe to eat and has been given an E number. Only very small amounts of colours are needed in a food.

> **In your coursework project you will need to:**
>
> - consider the use of different coloured ingredients to enhance the appearance and **aesthetic** properties of your food product
> - include a description of the expected colour of your product when you are writing out your **design brief** and in your **product specification**
> - consider the use of **quality assurance (QA)** procedures to ensure that the colour of your finished product matches the description in your product specification.

Coursework checkpoint: *colour*

You can investigate the way in which colour affects how much we like a product.

- Make a row of coloured sweets, one of each colour.
- Ask a range of people in your **target market group** which is their favourite colour.
- Ask the same people what colour vegetables they think make a meal look appealing.
- List the most popular colours for sweets and for vegetables.
- Explain any similarities and any differences in the choices made.

composite products are finished products, sold by **manufacturers** to be used as ingredients by the purchaser. They are not finished foods, ready for eating when they are sold. Composite products include frozen **pastry**, stock cubes, baking powder and pizza bases. They are very widely used in the catering industry, as well as being sold to the public in supermarkets.

computer-aided design (CAD) involves the use of computer hardware and design software to model ideas in 2D or 3D on the computer screen. CAD **modelling** is a key part of the industrial design process because it enables **manufacturers** to test and modify ideas quickly. This reduces the need for producing a wide range of product samples, saving time and costs.

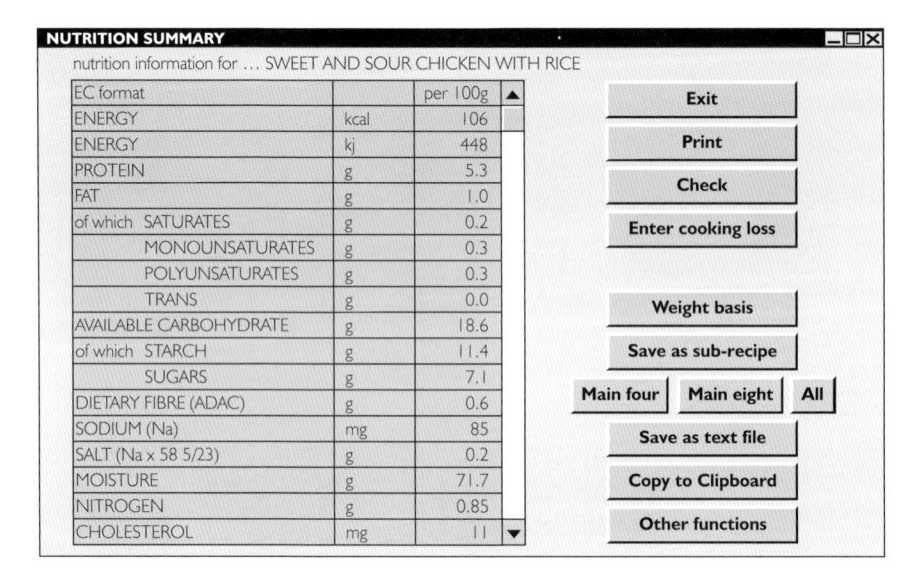

> **In your coursework project you will need to use:**
>
> - graphic techniques to generate and develop design ideas
> - CAD to develop and model design proposals
> - CAD to produce an accurate drawing of your **packaging design**
> - software to design and model on screen, to present work, produce **specification** sheets and model costs (simulate production methods).

NUTRITION SUMMARY		
nutrition information for ... SWEET AND SOUR CHICKEN WITH RICE		
EC format		per 100g
ENERGY	kcal	106
ENERGY	kj	448
PROTEIN	g	5.3
FAT	g	1.0
of which SATURATES	g	0.2
MONOUNSATURATES	g	0.3
POLYUNSATURATES	g	0.3
TRANS	g	0.0
AVAILABLE CARBOHYDRATE	g	18.6
of which STARCH	g	11.4
SUGARS	g	7.1
DIETARY FIBRE (ADAC)	g	0.6
SODIUM (Na)	mg	85
SALT (Na x 58 5/23)	g	0.2
MOISTURE	g	71.7
NITROGEN	g	0.85
CHOLESTEROL	mg	11

This software provides an easy and efficient way to create a label for a food package

Manufacturers can use CAD in various ways to:
- fit machinery into a factory layout
- help design heat processes (checks will always be necessary. Foods are natural products and don't always behave exactly as predicted.)
- calculate nutritional data for a recipe, to be placed on a **label**
- calculate the effects of making recipe changes
- design packaging
- model **shelf life** (again, checks are always necessary).

The use of **Information and Communication Technology (ICT)** enables CAD information to be sent electronically between manufacturers and their **clients**, so that design decisions can be made quickly.

> **Coursework checkpoint:** *computer-aided design (CAD)*
> - Use a digital camera to photograph your product. Then edit the photo to produce a picture as part of your packaging design.
> - You can photograph your product on its own or with other foods on a plate, if that is appropriate.
> - Remember, if you show any food that is not part of your product then you must include the words 'serving suggestion' on the picture when it is part of the packaging.

computer-aided manufacture (CAM) involves the use of computer systems to control manufacturing equipment, making it quicker, easier and cheaper to produce food products. CAM automates production so that fewer people are needed to operate machinery. Processes can be repeated easily and precisely. CAM is used extensively in a modern food factory with **batch, high volume,** or **continuous production**.

The uses of CAM include:

- the measuring of liquids (**metering**); weighing of ingredients; and controlling **mixing**
- controlling the temperature and time needed for **heat processing** such as cooking, baking, **canning** and **pasteurisation**
- packing, including the automatic weighing of food into packs
- cleaning food manufacturing machinery using a computerised cleaning programme. This means that the machinery does not have to be taken to pieces to be cleaned. This system is called Cleaning-in-Place (CIP).

Coursework checkpoint: *computer-aided manufacture (CAM)*
- You could make bread using a bread making machine.
- Draw a **flow chart** showing the operations carried out by the machine.
- Describe the advantages of using a bread making machine, compared to making bread by hand.

In your coursework project you will need to:

- understand how CAM is used in making **one-off**, batch and high volume products.

computer integrated manufacturing (CIM) systems integrate the use of all the different functions of computers, including **computer-aided design (CAD)** and **computer-aided manufacture (CAM)**, to enable fast, efficient and cost-effective manufacturing.

In food manufacturing CIM systems make use of CAD/CAM for product development (PD), the **modelling** of **packaging designs**, production planning, production operations, **quality control (QC)** and stock control.

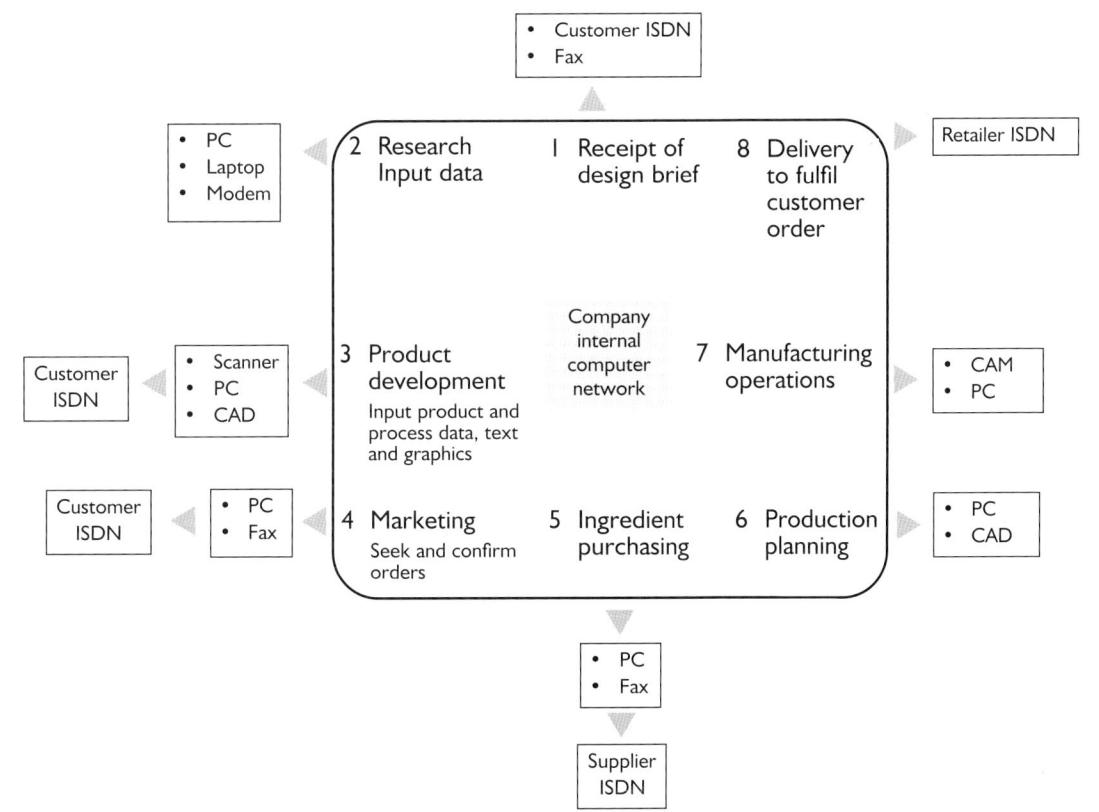

This diagram shows how a CIM system can integrate the use of different functions of computers

Understanding Industrial Practices: Food Technology © Nelson Thornes 2005

> **Coursework checkpoint:** *computer integrated manufacturing (CIM)*
>
> As a developer-maker you have to manage concurrent product development and manufacture, so you know how complicated it can be! You have the advantage that you don't generally need to communicate much information to other people during **one-off** manufacture.
>
> If you take part in **batch production** of a food product you will need to manage concurrent production as a team.
>
> - Work out when you can use CAD/CAM and what for.
> - Include all the technical and organisational information about the product in your **production plan**.
> - Use a computer network to share information, so that any team member making a change can communicate this to others in the team.

> **In your coursework project you will need to understand that:**
>
> ■ computer systems are used in the food industry to control manufacture
>
> ■ systems are made up of inputs, processes and outputs.

computer systems are used in industry for production planning, data control, computer-aided design (CAD), computer-aided manufacture (CAM), and Information and Communication Technology (ICT). The use of high-cost computer systems has revolutionised the manufacture of food products.

Computer systems are used by **manufacturers** because they are adaptable and accurate. They provide easy access to data storage and cost-effective, fast, high **quality** production. The use of computer systems can also reduce the need for people to do tedious, repetitive work. This can lead to unemployment unless other types of jobs become available.

The food industry uses computers for general activities such as:

- administration; calculating staff pay
- managing data about products, **raw materials**, components and stock. **Product Data Management (PDM)** systems can be used for this.
- planning production and **quality assurance (QA)**
- electronic communications between companies and **clients**, using ICT
- **costing**, accounts and **marketing**.

Specialist computer systems are used in food manufacturing for:

- calculating **nutritional information** for a recipe
- keeping track of ingredients as they move around the factory
- ensuring a steady flow of ingredients to a **continuous production** line
- controlling machinery and processes, including, for example, measuring of ingredients, **mixing**, **heat processing**, freezing time and freezer temperature.

General and specialist computer systems are made up of INPUT, PROCESS and OUTPUT activities.

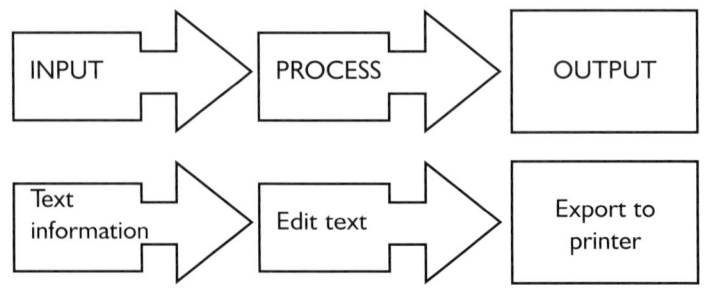

INPUT → PROCESS → OUTPUT

Text information → Edit text → Export to printer

Block diagram to show an example of a general computer system activity

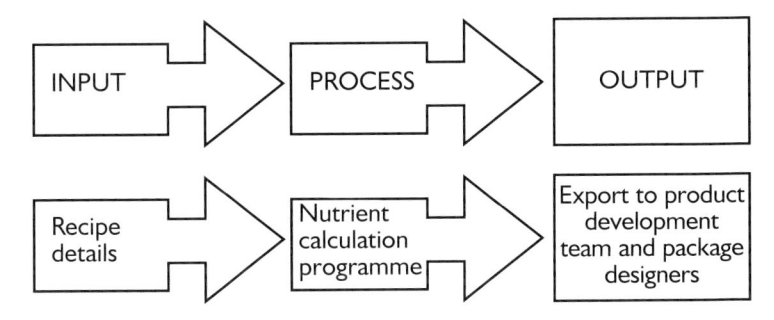

```
INPUT  ⇒  PROCESS  ⇒  OUTPUT

Recipe details  ⇒  Nutrient calculation programme  ⇒  Export to product development team and package designers
```

Block diagram to show an example of a specialist computer system activity

5 **continuous production** (continuous flow) can be used to manufacture basic food products, such as **flour**, crisps and bread. This type of production is highly automated. In other industries continuous production lines can operate 24 hours a day, every day, but in the food industry they must be stopped at regular intervals for cleaning, to maintain product and factory **hygiene** standards.

6 **control systems** can be electrical, electronic, mechanical or computer controlled. Control systems are used in manufacturing to control **batch**, **high volume** and **continuous production** systems. Control systems include:

- computer control (automation, computer-aided design/computer-aided manufacture (CAD/CAM), computer numerical control (CNC), Information and Communication Technology (ICT))
- integrated manufacturing systems (**computer integrated manufacturing (CIM), Product Data Management (PDM)**)
- quality control (QC) systems
- safety systems: **health and safety (H&S)** procedures, **risk assessment** and **Hazard Analysis Critical Control Point (HACCP)** are used to control safety for workers and **consumers**.
- stock control systems

Control systems consist of a co-ordinated arrangement of activities working together during which INPUTS are PROCESSED to achieve OUTPUTS.

In computer control, for example, the inputs could be the nett weight of food in packages of finished products from one production run. The weights are input automatically from a checkweigher. The process would be the calculation of the average weight of food in the packages and the output could be a print out of weight data, showing conformance to legal requirements. This is an example of a simple system that doesn't have any **feedback**, so it is called an open loop system.

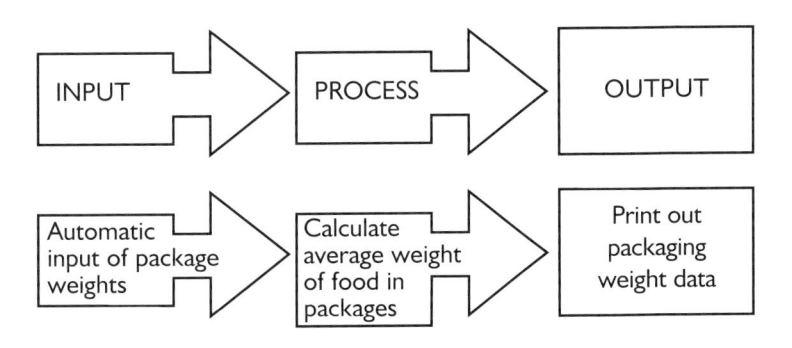

In your coursework project you will need to:

- choose the most suitable **method of production** for your food product and give reasons for choosing it
- understand what is meant by continuous production, why it is used for manufacturing products and how it compares with other methods of production
- understand how **quality control (QC)** techniques are used to manufacture high **quality** products.

In your coursework project you will need to:

- understand that a control system is made up of inputs, processes and outputs
- design and model your products on screen using computer control
- use a quality control system that incorporates feedback so your product complies with its **specification**
- use a safety system when manufacturing your product so your working environment is safe and the product is safe for the consumer.

```
INPUT  ⇒  PROCESS  ⇒  OUTPUT

Automatic input of package weights  ⇒  Calculate average weight of food in packages  ⇒  Print out packaging weight data
```

Block diagram of an open loop system showing computer control with no feedback

Control systems incorporate feedback of information to make different processes function well. A **flour** mill, for example, can incorporate feedback from sensors that will check the level of **protein** in the flour. If the protein is too low then the level will be automatically adjusted. A control system that incorporates feedback is called a closed loop system.

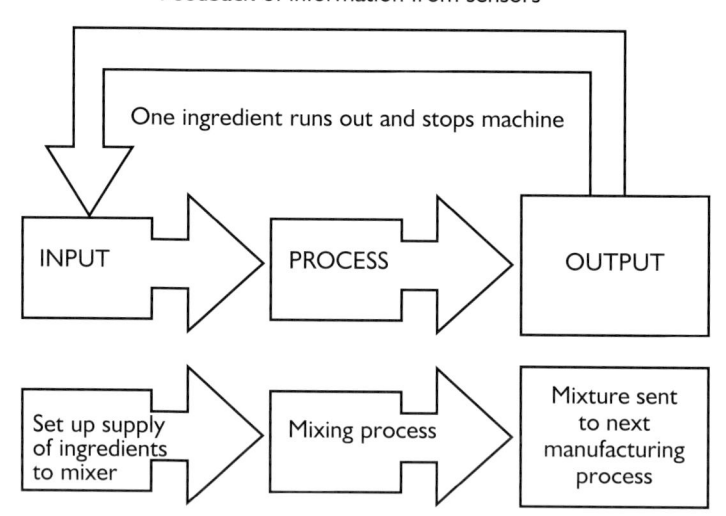

Block diagram of a closed loop system showing computer control with feedback

Many control systems used in food manufacturing incorporate feedback of information to make the manufacturing process work well. For example:

1. Materials handling systems such as automatic overhead conveyors are used to move chicken carcasses around a processing factory, so they are in the right place at the right time.
2. Manufacturing systems include the automated **pasteurisation** of milk.
3. Computer control systems are used to work out the flow of ingredients on to a **continuous production** line.
4. Electronic or computer control of processes includes the formation of, filling, heat-sealing and date coding of food packages.
5. Quality control systems use feedback from sensors to ensure the manufacture of high **quality** products.
6. Process control includes using temperature and time control to ensure a product receives adequate **heat processing**.
7. Safety systems in the food industry use feedback from sensors to prevent machinery from working if the correct safety guards are not in place.

Control systems are used in food manufacturing to:

- provide feedback that makes processes more reliable and safe
- repeat processes easily to make consistent products
- improve quality by enabling accurate work
- speed up production
- automate tedious processes
- reduce waste.

costing is the process of producing an accurate price for a product which will make it saleable *and* create a profit. **Manufacturers** have to cost their food products very accurately and this can be quite complicated, so **computer systems** are being used more widely for estimating costs and forecasting profits.

Costing can be done in set stages and needs to include the following:

1 DIRECT COSTS, such as materials and labour.
2 OVERHEAD COSTS, such as rent, heat, electricity, water and transport, which are often worked out as a set percentage of labour costs for a factory. Electricity and transport costs will be higher for chilled and frozen products.
3 MANUFACTURING COSTS, made up of direct and overhead costs.
4 MANUFACTURING PROFIT, worked out as a set percentage of manufacturing costs.
5 The SELLING PRICE, made up of the manufacturing costs and the manufacturing profit.

In your coursework project you will need to:

- choose a suitable **method of production** so your product is cost-effective to make
- use computer software, such as a spreadsheet, to model the cost of the materials and components used in your product.

1 **Direct costs** for a fresh, chilled, pre-packed fruit salad (200g).		
a) Materials		
Selection of prepared fruits @ £1.00 per kilo (average price)	£0.20	
Packaging (plastic tray + label)	£0.024	
Total cost of materials		£0.224
b) Labour		
0.05 hours at £5.60 per hour	£0.28	
Total cost of labour		£0.28
Total DIRECT COSTS		£0.504

2 **Overhead costs** can be worked out as a percentage of the labour costs.		
If percentage of the labour cost	= 20%	
Overhead cost	= 20% x £0.28	
	= £0.056	
Total OVERHEAD COSTS		£0.056

3 **Manufacturing costs** of fruit salad.		
Direct costs	£0.504	
Overhead costs	£0.056	
Total MANUFACTURING COSTS		£0.56

4 **Manufacturing profit** can be worked out as a set percentage of the manufacturing costs.		
If set percentage	= 60%	
Profit	= 60% x manufacturing costs	
	= 60% x £0.56	
	= £0.336	
Total MANUFACTURING PROFIT		£0.336

Understanding Industrial Practices: Food Technology © Nelson Thornes 2005

5 **Selling price** of fruit salad.		
Manufacturing costs	£0.560	
Manufacturing profit	£0.336	
SELLING PRICE to retail outlet		£0.896

Stages 1–5 on page 15 and above show the costing process for a simple fruit salad. How much would you have to pay for the fruit salad in the shops?

Reducing costs:
In the food industry the highest costs are usually the labour costs. The selling price of foods could be lowered by:

- using more **automation**
- using less expensive ingredients and packaging
- reducing the profit.

cook-chill is a system of catering where food is first prepared using conventional cooking methods. It is divided up into meal-sized portions and placed in oven-proof containers. The containers must then be chilled very quickly down to 0–3°C in order to maintain the **quality** of the food.

The food can be kept refrigerated for up to five days. When it is heated for eating it is important that the food reaches a temperature of at least 75°C, (Scottish law gives a temperature of 82°C) right to its centre, to be certain that no **pathogens** can survive in it. The **manufacturer** provides clear guidelines for cooking times and temperatures to make sure the food is safe and these should be followed by the **consumer**.

cook-freeze foods are prepared in the same way as **cook-chill**, except that the food is kept frozen. For this reason, cook-freeze meals will have a longer **shelf life** than cook-chill meals. Cook-freeze foods can be kept for up to 8 weeks without any noticeable loss of **taste** or loss of nutrients.

> **In your coursework project you will need to:**
>
> - identify CCPs in your manufacturing process
> - use **quality control (QC)** at CCPs to check the quality of your product against the **manufacturing process specification**.

a **critical control point (CCP)** is a stage in the manufacturing process that has been identified during the Hazard Analysis Critical Control Point (HACCP) evaluation. Operations carried out at a CCP must be controlled, to be sure that the food will be safe and of acceptable **quality** for the **consumer**. The control measures taken at a CCP must be monitored to make sure they are being carried out correctly.

> **Coursework checkpoint:** *critical control point (CCP)*
>
> The storage of raw and cooked foods is an example of a CCP. In industry, raw and cooked products are kept in different areas of the factory to avoid any risk of cross-contamination. In the home, raw meat should always be stored below cooked foods. Check your fridge at school and at home regularly to make sure foods are correctly stored. Record your findings on a record sheet such as the one below.

Date	Time	Storage checked	Any action taken	Name of QC technician
20.6	09.45	Raw pork chops in fridge; trifle on shelf above	None	Lee

Table 1 Record sheet

custom made (one-off) means designing and making a product specially to a client's requirements. This type of product might be a wedding cake, for example. Every custom-made product is different from all others. This type of food production is very labour-intensive and so products are more expensive than those made by other **methods of production**.

a **design brief** is a set of instructions given to a **product development team** by a **client**. The design brief needs to be simple and concise, explaining what needs to be done. It should include relevant details but not the solution to the problem. The design brief is used to plan **market research** and to start a **product development** (PD) project. The client (who could be your teacher) will often discuss the brief with the food product developer (product designer), who needs to be clear about what needs to be done.

Example of a design brief:
'A manufacturer wants to develop a new range of fillings for jacket potatoes to appeal to teenagers. Design a range of fillings that could be made and sold fresh in school.'

The design brief explains:

- what needs to be designed (a type of filling to be sold as a fresh, i.e. chilled, product)
- who the product is for (the **target market group**, such as teenagers at school)
- what the product will be used for (eaten as part of lunch or a snack. To be paid for by students, who have limited money available).

When you write a design brief and plan your research you will also need to consider when the product is required and how many of the products are needed. Will the products be suitable for **batch** or **high volume** production? When you research your target market group you will also need to think about where the products might be sold. The **quality** and cost needs of your intended target market will influence the retail market for your product. Remember, it is better to develop a simple product so you can meet the deadline for your coursework project.

> **Coursework checkpoints: *design brief***
>
> 1 In the Full Course GCSE in Design and Technology you may need to develop your own design brief based on a project outline given to you by your teacher. It is important to talk to your teacher to make sure that your design brief will enable you to cover all the coursework assessment criteria.
>
> Example of a Full Course project outline:
> You have been commissioned by a local factory to develop a range of filling soups, with suitable bread-based accompaniments, to be served in their work's canteen. The soups should be inspired by an Oriental theme. If your recipes are approved you may be asked to produce them in quantity. You are to make up one soup and one bread-based accompaniment.

In your coursework project you will need to:

- choose the most suitable method of production for your food product and give reasons for your choice
- understand what is meant by one-off production, why it is used for manufacturing products and how it compares with other methods of production
- understand that using **standard components** can make manufacturing more cost-effective
- understand how **quality control (QC)** is used to manufacture a high **quality** product.

In your coursework project you will need to:

- develop and use a design brief to develop a product
- use the design brief to plan research
- use the design brief to help develop a **design specification**.

Understanding Industrial Practices: Food Technology © Nelson Thornes 2005

2 In the Short Course GCSE in Design and Technology you are likely to be presented with a more focused project outline. It is important to talk to your teacher to make sure that your design brief will enable you to cover all of the coursework assessment criteria.

Example of a Short Course project outline:
You have been commissioned by a local factory to develop and make a filling soup inspired by Indian cuisine. If your soup is approved you may be asked to produce it in quantity to be sold in their work's canteen.

3 In GCSE Manufacturing you will be *given* a design brief that tells you the client's requirements. The client could be your teacher or someone from industry.

Example of a GCSE Manufacturing design brief:
Morasco, a major supermarket chain, are looking for a new 'healthy' pizza to sell in their stores next autumn. Initial market research has shown that a pizza base made including wholemeal flour, with low-fat cheese in the topping would be popular. The pizza should be the right size for a single serving. The development prototype should be completed by 1 March.

In your coursework project you will need to:

- develop and use detailed design specification criteria
- use your design specification to generate design ideas
- test and evaluate your design ideas by comparing them to your design specification
- use your design specification and final design proposal to develop a **product specification**
- use your design specification and product specification to develop a **manufacturing process specification**.

---

a **design specification** is developed from the design brief and includes information about the design and manufacture of the product. Key features of the design brief are selected and then researched to find detailed information about each one. This information is then used to write design specification criteria stating:

- the purpose of the product, including its nutritional value
- the requirements and size of the **target market group** – so the product will reflect the needs of the **consumer**
- what the product should look like – its **aesthetic** characteristics
- how it should be packaged – this will affect the **shelf life** of the product
- how it should be manufactured, e.g. ingredients needed, their costs, seasonal availability
- production details, e.g. processing operations required, equipment needed or manufacturing skills required
- **quality** standards for the product, e.g. its weight and shape, including **tolerances**, product finish and packaging
- safety requirements – how to ensure its safe manufacture and use
- how much it might cost.

Coursework checkpoint: *design specification*

○ Your design specification can sometimes change slightly as you research your product.
○ Remember to evaluate your design ideas against your design specification criteria.
○ Use your design specification criteria and your final design proposal to help develop your product specification. This provides all the information about the product.

In GCSE Design and Technology the design specification is developed from the design brief and research. It helps you generate and evaluate your design ideas, monitor the effectiveness of your design work and develop a product specification and a manufacturing process specification.

In GCSE Manufacturing the product design specification helps you develop initial ideas for what the product will be like, how the product could be manufactured and how much it might cost. The product design specification needs to include criteria related to any relevant nutritional requirements and cost of appropriate ingredients, the most cost-effective way to manufacture the product, quality and safety standards. You will need to use **feedback** from your **client** to help develop your final design proposal.

designing for manufacture means designing a food product that meets a **design brief**. This is **product development (PD)** and in industry it is the work of the **product development team**. A **manufacturing process specification** is drawn up to guide the manufacturing process so that the product is the same every time it is made.

When designing for manufacture, you need to take into account the following:

- What the product should be like.
- The scale of production.
- The availability and cost of **raw materials** and equipment.
- The manufacturing processes and ease of production.
- The skills required to manufacture the product.
- The expected cost and **quality** of the product.
- How to make the product on time and at a reasonable cost.

Coursework checkpoint: *designing for manufacture*

Make sure that you design your food product so that it is easy to manufacture. You may need to:

○ simplify the design or making processes
○ make the best use of ingredients and reduce waste
○ use processes that can easily be repeated
○ check you have the skills you need to manufacture your product
○ identify where and how you will check for quality
○ work out a **costing** for the product
○ make sure that you can make your product in the time available.

In your coursework project you will need to:
■ choose the most suitable **method of production** for your product and give reasons for choosing it
■ design a food product that could be manufactured in quantity
■ understand what is meant by **batch production**, why it is used for manufacturing products and how it compares with other methods of production
■ match food ingredients with tools, equipment and processes
■ produce and use a detailed work schedule which shows the processes needed to manufacture your product, in their correct order
■ make sure that the quality of your product is appropriate for your **target market group**
■ work to realistic deadlines.

Dietary Reference Values (DRV)

is a collective term used to cover the Reference Nutrient Intake (RNI) and Estimated Average Requirements (EAR). These are guideline values to the need for certain nutrients. They are set for people in different age/sex groups by the Department of Health.

drying

is a heat process that is used to preserve some foods. The aim in drying is to remove moisture from the food rather than to kill **micro-organisms**. These cannot grow in dried foods because there is no water for them and so the food does not spoil. Other forms of **heat processing**, such as **pasteurisation** or **sterilisation** of milk, are used to kill micro-organisms.

The **packaging material** used for dried foods such as soup mixes and powdered milk is very important. It must prevent any moisture from reaching the food while it is being stored. Dried foods have some advantages over other forms of preserved foods.

- They weigh less and take up less room because the water has been removed. This makes them very suitable for round-the-world sailors or for the armed forces on exercise.
- Dried foods are cheaper to transport because they weigh less.
- They have a very long **shelf life**, provided they are kept cool and dry.

The **quality** of dried foods is judged by how closely they resemble the original food when they have been rehydrated. Food can be dried using:

1. Sun drying, which is a traditional way of drying that can be used only in hot countries. It has the big advantage that the energy to provide the heat is free! The disadvantage of drying food in the open air is that birds and other pests can contaminate it.

2. Spray drying, which is used to produce dried, powdered foods, such as milk powder or coffee whitener. Liquid milk is fed slowly into the top of the spray drier through an atomiser that rotates at very high speed. This changes the liquid into a very fine spray. Hot air in the drier chamber makes the water in this fine spray evaporate, leaving behind the dried milk powder.

   When it leaves the spray drier, the milk powder is very difficult to rehydrate, so it then goes through a process called instantising. The powder is made slightly wet; enough to make several particles of powder stick together. It is then dried again. The larger clumps of powder are very easy to rehydrate.

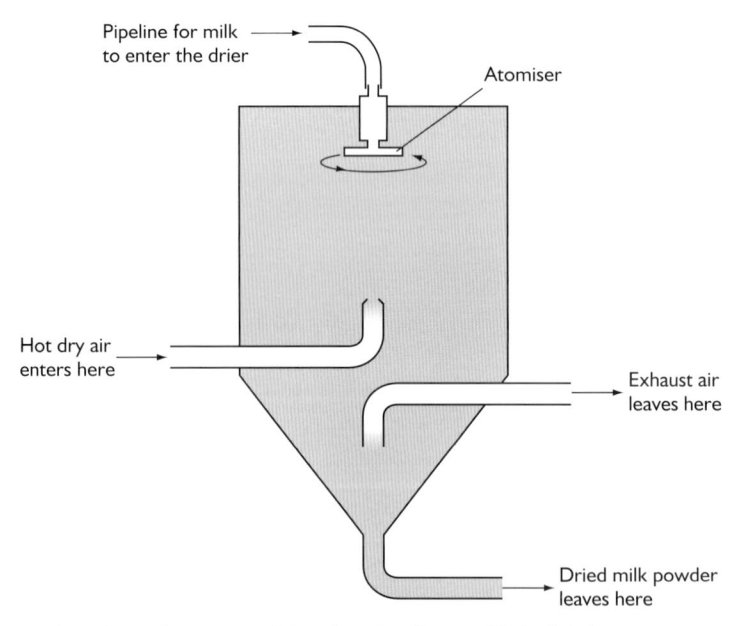

Cross-section through a spray drier showing how milk is dried

> **Coursework checkpoint: *drying***
> - Check out the effects of drying on fruit by examining dried fruit pieces and comparing them with fresh fruits.
> - Try making your own muesli mix using dried fruits. Then make a similar mix using fresh fruits. Draw up a table giving the advantages and disadvantages of each product to the **consumer**.

eggs are a **primary food** with a high nutritional value. Before retail sale they must be inspected to ensure they are not cracked and then they are graded for size. Eggs are also used as an ingredient in many **secondary foods**, such as cakes, quiches and some types of pasta.

Many secondary food **manufacturers** buy liquid egg, which consists of eggs that have been de-shelled and blended together. Liquid egg must, by law, be pasteurised before it is used. Using liquid egg saves manufacturers having to handle all the egg-shells. It can also be **metered** into a mixer rather than having to be weighed out, so it is far simpler and cleaner to use than eggs in their shells. Manufacturers also use powdered egg. This is produced by spray **drying** and is used in foods such as cake mixes and batter mixes.

Egg has some useful **functional properties** that make it useful as a food ingredient, in addition to providing nutritional value.

1. Whole egg is used:
   - as a binder in products, such as potato croquettes and in food coatings
   - as a glazing agent for pies and tarts, giving them an attractive golden-brown colour.
2. Egg yolks can be used as an **emulsifier**.
3. Egg white can be used to produce foams, for meringues, soufflés and mousses. It is also used as a binder for Quorn™.

Electronic Point of Sale (EPOS) tills collect information about the sales of food products from shops and supermarkets. This data is sorted by computer and stock levels are calculated. Orders are sent, via electronic links, to suppliers for quick delivery of fast selling items. EPOS tills are used in **Information and Communication Technology (ICT)** systems, which enable retailers and **manufacturers** to respond quickly to customer demand. If a food product is selling very well, the manufacturer may have to produce more to fulfil the demand.

the **e mark** is found beside the weight declaration on food packages. It means that the packages may be sold in any country in the EU without the importer having to check the net weight of the contents to make sure they comply with EU law. The e mark is not compulsory; packages that do not show it are intended for sale only in the country where they are packed.

A food label showing the e mark

an **emulsifier** is used to help two liquids, such as oil and water, stay mixed together instead of separating out from one another. Examples of emulsifiers include:
- egg yolk, used in salad cream
- soya lecithin, used in some instant desserts
- monoglycerides/diglycerides of fatty acids, used in margarine.

Coursework checkpoint: *emulsifier*

You can observe the effect of an emulsifier on an oil and water mix.

- Take two test tubes and pour 5cm³ of water into each one. Then add 5cm³ of cooking oil to each tube.

- Add a few drops of liquid egg yolk to one tube only.
- Place a stopper over each tube and shake them both vigorously for 15 seconds.
- Place the tubes in a rack and immediately make a note of what you see in each tube.
- Make a further note about what you see after 2 minutes and again after 5 minutes.

an **emulsion** is a stable mixture of two liquids, such as oil and water, that would not normally stay mixed together. To form an emulsion, such as in salad cream, the oil must be broken down into very small droplets which can be dispersed evenly throughout the vinegar and water used in the recipe. In salad cream an **emulsifier** (**egg** yolk) and a **stabiliser** (Xanthan gum) are used to prevent the oil droplets from coming back together and reforming into a separate layer.

Butter, margarine, ice-cream and milk are also examples of food products that contain emulsions.

enrobing can be used to coat biscuits with chocolate or to coat foods such as fish or chicken pieces before cooking. Common coatings are made using either a batter mix or with breadcrumbs. Beaten **egg** or batter can be used to help breadcrumbs stick to the food. The **colour** of the crumbs can be chosen to enhance the **appearance** of the food.

Enrobing can be used to introduce a wide variety of different flavourings into food. It can also provide a textural contrast on the outside to the **texture** of the food inside. Enrobed products are known as value-added foods as they sell for a higher price than the same product would without a coating.

In your coursework project you will need to:

- understand that combining food ingredients can enhance the **aesthetic** properties and value of foods
- cut, shape, combine and process ingredients to create more desirable food products.

Coursework checkpoint: *enrobing*

Check out an enrobed product such as a fish finger.
- What ingredients are used in the coating?
- What percentage of the fish finger is actually fish?
- Investigate how you could produce a value-added fish product using enrobing.

environmental issues affect all industries, but there are some special concerns for the food industry.

1. Disposal of waste:
   Food waste must be disposed of in an approved way. This can include the disposal of materials such as offal from animals, washing water from cleaning and peeling vegetables and waste from spillages within the factory. Waste cooking oil from factories such as fish finger **manufacturers** and from fast food outlets must be removed by licensed companies.

2. Reduction in energy use:
   Food manufacturing operations, such as **canning** and baking, use large amounts of energy. In many cases energy-recycling schemes have been introduced, so that the heat is used again, rather than being lost to the air outside the factory. This can give significant cost savings to the factory as well as reducing usage of fuel.

3. Reduction in the use of **packaging materials**:
   Food must be packaged in suitable packaging materials.

In your coursework project you will need to:

- consider the needs of the environment when developing your product **design specification**
- use safe manufacturing processes and packaging materials that reduce risks to the environment
- take account of waste **raw materials** when designing and making your product.

Biodegradable packaging materials are not suitable for packaging in contact with food, as these could cause stored foods to leak or become unsafe.

4 Recycling:
Recycled paper and board can be used for outer food containers, but not for those that come into direct contact with food. Most food packaging materials are recyclable. Aluminium and steel cans, for example, give guidance to the **consumer** about recycling. The government has set targets for recycling packaging materials that both manufacturers and retailers must achieve.

5 Factory cleanliness:
Keeping the grounds around the factory clean is essential to prevent pests such as rats, mice, birds and insects being attracted to the area.

6 Reduction in the use of fertilisers and pesticides:
There is concern about soil pollution and its effects on human health and wildlife. The use of pesticides has been greatly reduced in the past few years. Food manufacturers, supermarket groups and government bodies regularly monitor pesticide levels in food.

7 Sustainable food production:
This is a global issue, making sure that the world's resources are not depleted for our needs. Examples include:
- the use of paper from sustainable forests for packaging
- the planting of trees for food crops, such as cocoa trees in Africa and south America, so as not to endanger the local environment
- fishing in a way that does not destroy other species, e.g. 'dolphin friendly' catching of tuna.

Coursework checkpoint: *environmental issues*

1 Follow safety regulations and instructions so you dispose of waste ingredients safely.

2 Use waste management principles in your food **product development (PD)**. Ask yourself these questions to help you help the environment:
- Can you design and make more efficiently?
- If you can't prevent waste, can you use it for something else?
- If you can't reuse waste, can you recycle it?

3 Don't forget that waste needs to be added to the cost of your food product development.

E numbers are given to food **additives** that have been approved for use within the EU. The additives are divided into categories, for example:
- Colours.
- Preservatives.
- Antioxidants.
- Emulsifiers.
- Stabilisers.
- Thickeners.
- Gelling agents.
- Sweeteners.

The **ingredients list** on the food label must show the category that the additive is placed in.

This ingredients list shows several different categories of additives

Manufacturers may choose to identify an additive by its E number rather than its name. This is useful if the name is long and complicated. E471 is listed as mono- and diglycerides of fatty acids.

enzymes are proteins that are found in all living matter. They are biological catalysts that speed up the rate of a reaction. Each enzyme is specific to a particular reaction so, for example, an enzyme that helps to break down the bonds within a protein molecule will have no effect on carbohydrates, or on fats. Enzymes are used in the production of cheese. This has to be allowed to ripen before it is ready to be eaten. During ripening, enzymes break down some of the bonds in the cheese protein molecules. This helps give cheese its distinctive flavour. It is an example of the use of biotechnology in food production.

Enzymes often need to be treated during food processing as they might cause browning or other changes within the food during storage. This can be done through heat treatment (blanching), by changing the pH of the food or by irradiation.

Estimated Average Requirement (EAR) refers to the requirements of a group of people for energy, protein, vitamins or minerals. These values are issued by the Department of Health. Because individuals vary, so do their needs for different nutrients. Half of the people in any group will usually need more than the EAR and half will need less.

Age (years)	Male (kcal/day)	Female (kcal/day)
1–3	1230	1165
4–6	1715	1545
11–14	2220	1845
15–18	2755	2111
19–50	2550	1940
65–74	2330	1900

Table 2 EAR values for energy, for some different age groups

fats and oils are present in nearly all food materials. Fats are solid at room temperature and oils are liquid. The chemical bonding within each fat or oil determines whether it is saturated or unsaturated. Fats come mainly from animal sources and are likely to contain more saturated fat than the oils that come mainly from vegetable sources.

- Fats do not melt at one specific temperature (like water does). They soften and melt over a temperature range. When they are soft they are easier to work and they are said to be plastic.
- Oils used in the manufacture of margarine, shortenings and other spreads have to undergo a process called hydrogenation. This changes them from liquid oils into solid fats. Different oils and fats can then be blended together so that the blended fat is soft at the required temperatures. Margarines and spreads that can be used straight from the fridge contain blended fats and oils that start to soften at very low temperatures.

Fats and oils have several functions in food:

- They provide **flavour**. Butter is used in some biscuits and **pastry** to give a 'richer' flavour to the product.
- They make food seem less dry in the mouth.
- They are a good medium for **heat transfer**, so they are widely used in food preparation, for frying or for basting.

Fats and oils may go rancid if they are left exposed to air. Rancidity is characterised by an unpleasant smell and **taste** of the food. **Antioxidants** can be added to food to slow the onset of rancidity.

Current health guidelines recommend that we reduce our intake of fats and oils, especially saturated fats. **Manufacturers** now make many 'low-fat' alternatives to their standard products to help **consumers** cut their fat intake.

feedback is when information is fed back into a system to make it work well. Feedback from **sensory analysis** is important in developing a new product that is liked by the **target market group**. During production, information about a process can be found using computer sensors or by observation and analysis by staff. Any necessary adjustments to the process may be made automatically by computer, or by a technician altering the amount of ingredients being used.

For example:

1. In one factory the level of acidity in a batch of tomato ketchup might be monitored automatically during production. If the sensors find a low acidity then the system will automatically adjust the amount of vinegar being used until it is right.

2. In another factory a **quality assurance (QA)** technician might measure the acidity of the ketchup as a QA test. If the acidity level is low the technician will have to get it adjusted before the batch can be released.

In your coursework project you will need to:

- incorporate feedback into your own design and manufacturing system
- use feedback from your **sensory panel**, **client** or target market group to help you modify and improve your design ideas.

fermentation is a process carried out by **micro-organisms**. In bread production, yeast ferments sugars to produce the gas that makes the bread rise. Fermentation can also be used to introduce new **tastes** into food and to increase its **shelf life**. For example, plain yoghurt is produced from milk, with no **flavour additives**, but it tastes very different to milk.

In the production of plain yoghurt, the milk is first heated at 90°C for 30 minutes to kill all micro-organisms. **Bacteria** are then added to the milk under controlled conditions. The bacteria ferment the lactose (**sugar**) in the milk, converting it to lactic acid. This helps the **proteins** in the milk to coagulate, which gives yoghurt its **texture**. The lactic acid also helps to preserve the yoghurt.

finishing processes, including **glazing**, garnishing, icing and piping, can be used to enhance the **aesthetic** properties of food. For example, a trifle with cream piped on to its top will have a different **appearance**, **taste** and **texture** to one made without the cream. In the same way, fresh herbs can be used to garnish a pizza.

In your coursework project you will need to:

- know about a variety of finishing processes
- know that product finishing processes can improve the aesthetic properties of food products.

Coursework checkpoint: *finishing processes*
Experiment with using finishing processes to enhance the **quality** of your product. For example, add a garnish using lemon and parsley to a fish dish, or try piping cream or icing in different designs on to the top of a cake.

---

the **fitness for purpose** of a product is evaluated through its performance, price and **aesthetic** appeal. A product that is fit for its purpose is well-designed and well-manufactured so that its **quality** meets the needs of the end user. The quality needs of the user are met by the product's:

- nutritional value – everyone needs food to supply them with essential nutrients. The nutritional value of the food should be suitable for the **target market group**.
- **appearance** and the image it gives the user – is the product well designed and attractive to the target market?
- performance in use – is the product well made using suitable ingredients? Is it good to eat?
- value for money – is the product made within budget limits to sell at an attractive price?

In your coursework project you will need to:

- evaluate the quality of your product to make sure that it is suitable for your intended user(s)
- modify your product where appropriate to improve its quality so it meets the needs of your target market group.

flavour makes food appetising and enjoyable. Food flavours are very complex, volatile compounds that produce vapours when the food is eaten. Flavour is detected by a mixture of **aroma** (by the nose) and taste buds (on the tongue). There are numerous flavouring products available to the **manufacturer** so that quite subtle flavours can be achieved when developing new products. For example, there are over 20 different flavoured varieties of crisps and similar snack products on sale in the UK.

flavour enhancers are used to alter **flavour** in some foods. The most common is monosodium glutamate (MSG) which occurs naturally in soy sauce. MSG 'brings out' meat and vegetable flavours but has little effect on sweet flavours. It is used primarily in canned and dried soups and in canned meats. MSG must only be used in very small amounts, as large amounts can cause dizziness and sickness.

flour is a primary food produced by the size reduction of wheat grains. The brown outer layers of the grain (bran) are removed and the white starchy interior (endosperm) is ground down to form a powder (flour). When wholemeal flour is produced the bran is included in the flour. Some **vitamins** and **minerals** are lost when white flour is made, so by law the flour miller has to add them to the white flour. Calcium carbonate is also added to white flour by law, so that foods containing flour are a good source of calcium in our diet. The addition of vitamins and minerals to foods is known as **fortification**.

The main component of flour is **starch**. Wheat flour also contains **proteins** that can join together to form a substance called gluten. Gluten can form a strong, elastic sheet of protein. This is used to trap the gas that is produced in the dough during bread making.

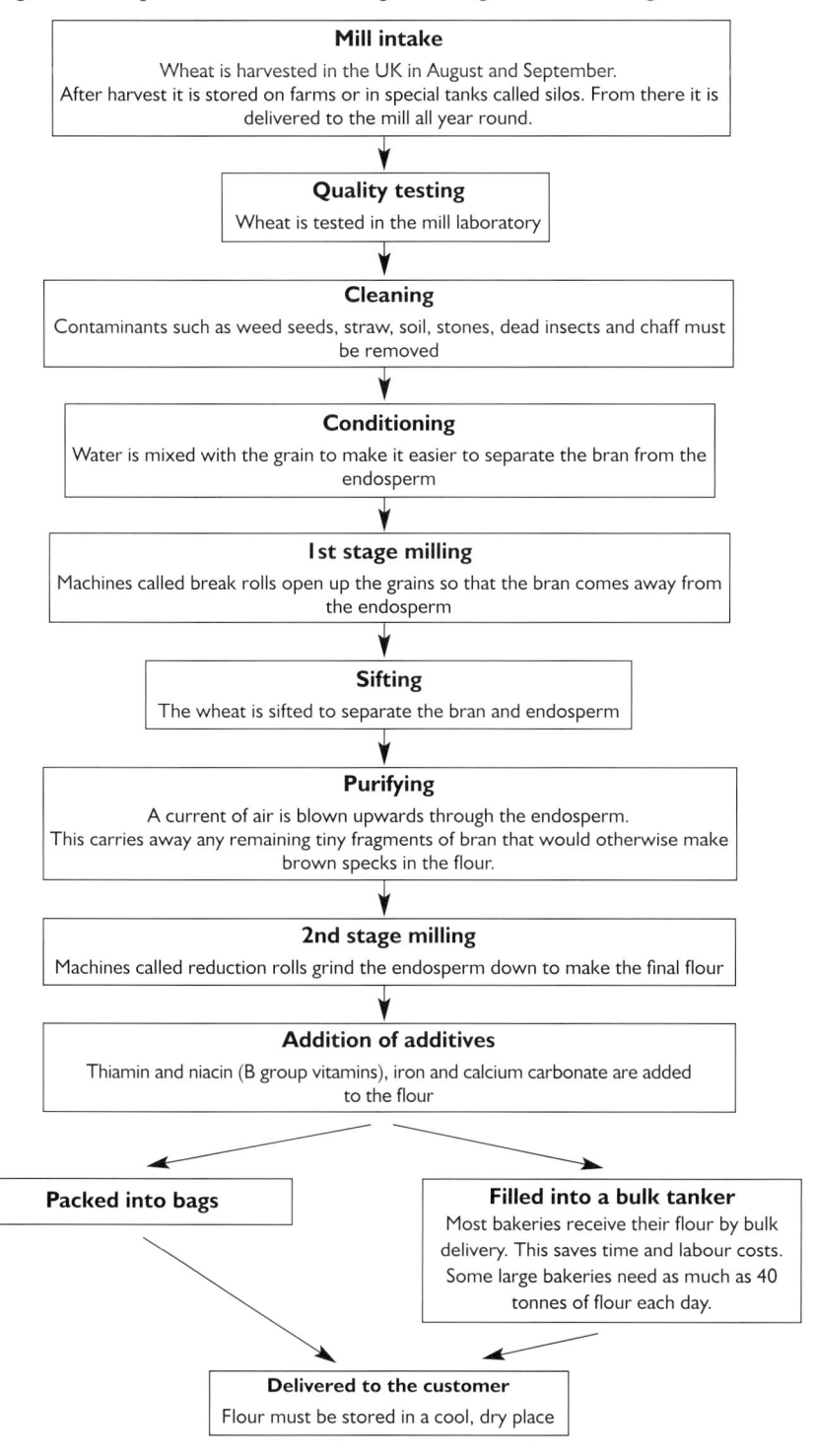

Mill intake
Wheat is harvested in the UK in August and September.
After harvest it is stored on farms or in special tanks called silos. From there it is delivered to the mill all year round.

↓

Quality testing
Wheat is tested in the mill laboratory

↓

Cleaning
Contaminants such as weed seeds, straw, soil, stones, dead insects and chaff must be removed

↓

Conditioning
Water is mixed with the grain to make it easier to separate the bran from the endosperm

↓

1st stage milling
Machines called break rolls open up the grains so that the bran comes away from the endosperm

↓

Sifting
The wheat is sifted to separate the bran and endosperm

↓

Purifying
A current of air is blown upwards through the endosperm.
This carries away any remaining tiny fragments of bran that would otherwise make brown specks in the flour.

↓

2nd stage milling
Machines called reduction rolls grind the endosperm down to make the final flour

↓

Addition of additives
Thiamin and niacin (B group vitamins), iron and calcium carbonate are added to the flour

↙ ↘

Packed into bags

Filled into a bulk tanker
Most bakeries receive their flour by bulk delivery. This saves time and labour costs. Some large bakeries need as much as 40 tonnes of flour each day.

↘ ↙

Delivered to the customer
Flour must be stored in a cool, dry place

How white flour is produced from wheat

Standard symbols used in a flow chart:
- Operation (circle)
- Inspection (square)
- Storage (triangle)
- Delay (D-shape)
- Transport (arrow)

A **flow chart** (flow diagram) is a convenient way of showing on paper all the stages in a manufacturing process. Flow charts can be used to plan where and how the **quality** of a product is checked.

- An *operation* is performed by an operator on a food material.
- An *inspection* is performed by an operator on a food material.
- *Storage* is of a food material.
- A *delay* holds up an operator or a food material.
- *Transport* is movement of an operator or of a food material.

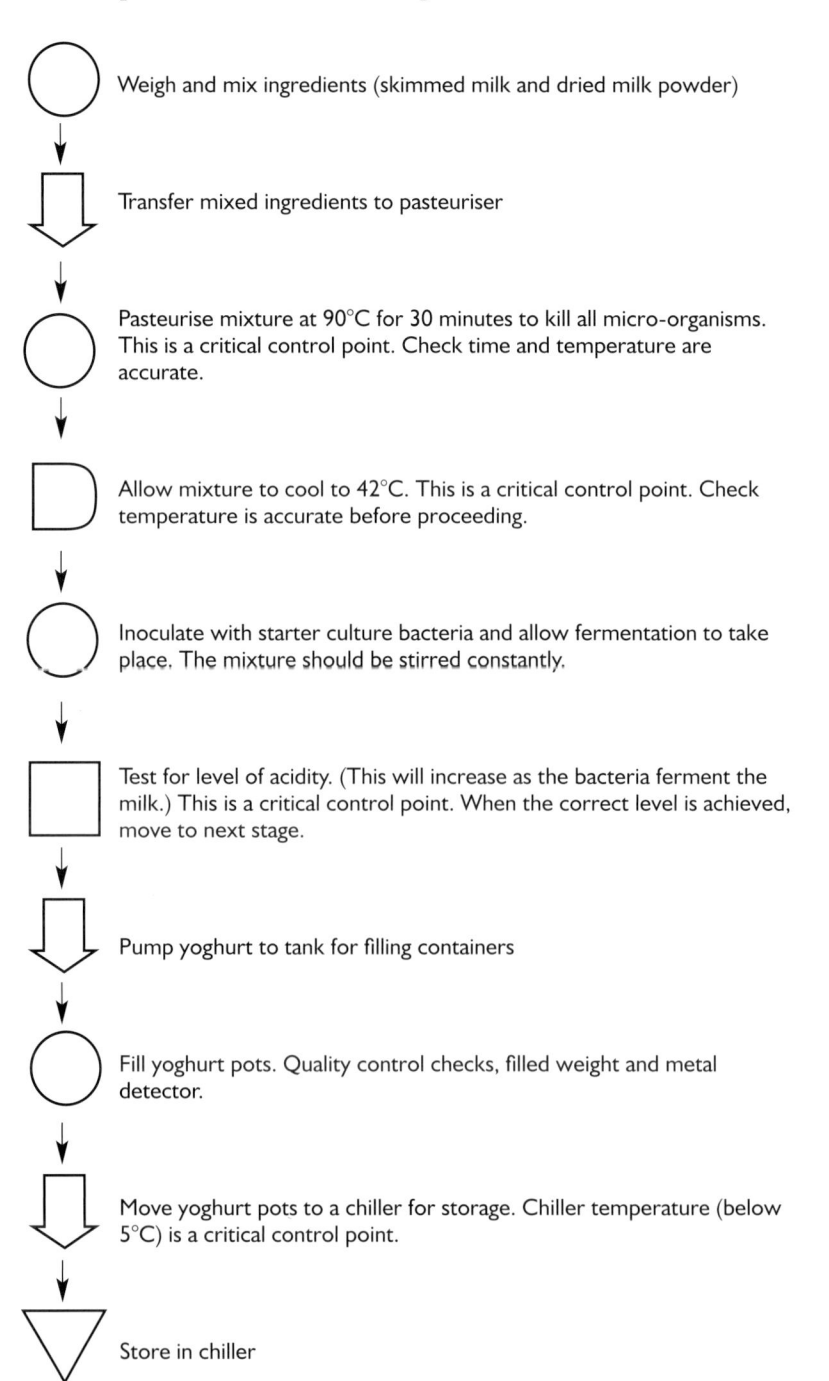

○ Weigh and mix ingredients (skimmed milk and dried milk powder)

⇩ Transfer mixed ingredients to pasteuriser

○ Pasteurise mixture at 90°C for 30 minutes to kill all micro-organisms. This is a critical control point. Check time and temperature are accurate.

D Allow mixture to cool to 42°C. This is a critical control point. Check temperature is accurate before proceeding.

○ Inoculate with starter culture bacteria and allow fermentation to take place. The mixture should be stirred constantly.

□ Test for level of acidity. (This will increase as the bacteria ferment the milk.) This is a critical control point. When the correct level is achieved, move to next stage.

⇩ Pump yoghurt to tank for filling containers

○ Fill yoghurt pots. Quality control checks, filled weight and metal detector.

⇩ Move yoghurt pots to a chiller for storage. Chiller temperature (below 5°C) is a critical control point.

▽ Store in chiller

Flow chart showing the production of low-fat yoghurt (simplified)

In your coursework project you will need to:

- produce and use a plan to show the stages of manufacture of your product
- incorporate **feedback** into your own design and manufacturing system.

Coursework checkpoint: *flow chart*

- Include a flow chart in your **manufacturing process specification** to show where and how you will check for quality. This will enable you to show the use of feedback from your quality checks.
- Using a flow chart with feedback loops will demonstrate your use of a **quality control (QC)** system.

food processing operations are carried out for a number of reasons:

1. To preserve food.
   When a food is harvested there is usually far too much to be eaten all at once. If the food is not preserved in some way to extend its **shelf life** it will spoil. Food preservation can be carried out at home, such as making jam from surplus fruit. **Freezing** can also be used to preserve surplus garden vegetables.

2. To increase consumer choice.
   Foods from all over the world are eaten in this country. Without processing and preservation it would be impossible for these foods to be imported without spoiling.

3. To increase variety in the diet.
   Processed foods are available all year round, so our diet need not be boring. The introduction of different **flavours** into foods increases **consumer** choice.

4. To convert basic ingredients into edible products and ingredients for secondary processing.
   Wheat, oil seeds and meat carcasses are not suitable foods in their original state. They need to be processed in order to provide food materials.

5. To provide convenience in shopping and eating.
   - Fresh foods have to be purchased frequently as they will not keep. Most people prefer to shop for food once a week. Processed foods can therefore save a lot of time. For example, ready-made sauces are easier and quicker to use than preparing them from basic ingredients.
   - Ready-meals, especially microwaveable ones, are also convenient for preparing quick, easy meals.

6. To add value to the food.
   Food ingredients generally sell at low prices, with very low profit margins. Mixing different ingredients together adds value and increases the profit margin for the **manufacturer**.

In your coursework project you will need to:

- think about food safety when planning the manufacture of your product
- follow hygiene rules when making food products
- use **Hazard Analysis Critical Control Point (HACCP)** to identify **critical control points (CCPs)** in the manufacture of your product
- work out and use QC procedures to effectively control and monitor your CCPs
- check the safety of your product, so it is safe for your intended consumers and the environment.

food safety is the top priority of all responsible food **manufacturers** and retailers. They have a legal and moral responsibility to make sure that food sold to the public will not cause illness or injury. All processes and procedures within the factory and supermarket are designed to ensure food safety.

Manufacturers must:

- use suitable processing conditions and **packaging materials**
- use appropriate **quality assurance (QA)** and **quality control (QC)** procedures
- ensure suitable **hygiene** standards within the factory
- ensure food is cleaned as necessary and that no contaminants enter the food while it is in the factory
- store and distribute food in hygienic conditions and at the correct temperature
- carry out **shelf life testing** and mark foods clearly with their correct 'use by' or 'best before' date.

Supermarkets must:

- make sure food cannot become contaminated while it is in the store
- ensure all chilled and frozen foods are kept at the correct temperatures
- make sure all food is removed from sale before it passes its 'use by' or 'best before' date.

Food manufacturers have a responsibility to recall foods from the shops and from **consumers** if a problem has occurred after the food has been delivered. Food packages are marked to show exactly what day and at what time they are packed. The **production line** in the factory can also be identified. In this way the manufacturers can give the exact code on any packages of food that need to be returned.

forming is used by meat, fish and vegetable **manufacturers** to make value-added products. Forming can convert spare trimmings of meat or fish into saleable products.

- The food material is placed in moulds.
- When the portions are released from the moulds they have a uniform **texture** and are the same size every time. This is useful for cost control for the manufacturer. It is also useful for the **consumer** as the product is always the same size and weight.
- Formed foods are often enrobed with a coating, usually of batter or breadcrumbs. Forming and **enrobing** can be used to increase the variety of foods available. Burgers and some cold meats are formed products, including, for example, sliced cold meat with a 'bear' shape in the middle. Examples of formed and coated products include fish cakes, potato croquettes and chicken nuggets.

In your coursework project you will need to understand that:

- combining materials create more useful properties
- materials can be cut, shaped, combined and processed to create more useful properties
- processes change the properties of materials.

Coursework checkpoint: *forming*

Design and make a formed and coated vegetable burger. Use mashed potato as the main ingredient and to bind it all together. You can form your product using a round biscuit cutter. Then coat it in a liquid batter. Finally, coat it with breadcrumbs. You will then have to fry it gently to 'fix' the coating.

fortification is the addition of nutrients such as **vitamins** or **minerals** to foods. There are two main reasons for this:

1. To replace nutrients lost during processing. For example, thiamin, niacin, iron and calcium carbonate are added to white **flour**. These must be added by law and do not need to be included on the **ingredients list**. Thiamin is also added to some breakfast cereals to replace the thiamin lost during manufacture due to the effects of heat.

2. To make sure the population get enough of nutrients they might otherwise lack. Vitamins A and D must, by law, be added to margarine, which is a product that nearly everyone eats. Iron and vitamins such as niacin, riboflavin and folic acid may also be added to some breakfast cereals.

freezing is used to preserve a wide range of foods, including fish and meat, fruits and vegetables, some dairy foods and baked products. Freezing causes fewer textural and nutritional changes to the food than other processing methods (e.g. **canning**; drying) so the food more closely resembles its fresh equivalent.

- Food must be frozen rapidly so that the water inside it forms only small ice crystals. Slow freezing allows the formation of large ice crystals that will be lost as 'drip loss' when the food is thawed. The **texture** of the food becomes tougher and dryer, as a result.
- **Bacteria** will not grow in frozen food, but may grow in thawed food, especially if left at room temperature. Frozen food should not be allowed to thaw until it is wanted for eating. If the freezer temperature fluctuates while the food is being stored, the eating **quality** of the food can be impaired.
- Freezers used in industry are just to freeze food. Once the food is frozen it is moved to a cold store, where it is kept frozen to await distribution. In an industrial cold store frozen foods have a very long **shelf life** because the temperature can be kept very low and very steady.

Manufacturers use different types of freezers, depending on the type and volume of product to be made. All types of freezers are available for either **batch** or **continuous production**.

1. A plate freezer is used for foods such as fish fillets or ready-meals that have been packed into thin boxes before freezing. A layer of boxes is loaded between two hollow metal plates that contain refrigerant. The plates press against the boxes so that there is maximum possible contact between them and the food freezes very fast.

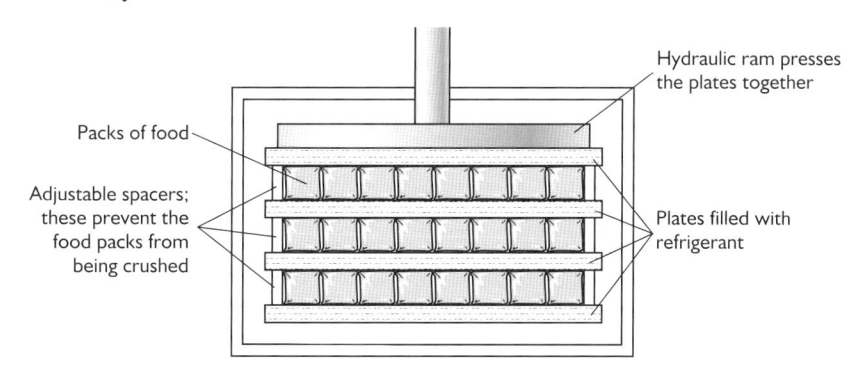

A diagram of a plate freezer showing how food packages are placed between the plates

2. A blast freezer is used for foods with an irregular shape, such as poultry and for delicate foods like cream cakes. Food is placed in a cabinet (for a batch process) where it is frozen by cold air passing all around it. A special type of blast freezer is the *spiral freezer* where food is placed on a conveyor belt that carries it continuously through the freezer in an upward spiral. The length of time the food spends in the freezer can be controlled by altering the speed of the belt, to make sure that the food is completely frozen. This type of freezer is very suitable for **high volume** production.

3. A fluidised bed freezer is useful for small items of food, like peas or Brussels sprouts. The food to be frozen flows along a mesh belt, or bed. A strong current of cold air is blasted up from underneath, so that the food is lifted up above the bed. The food pieces are frozen separately (known as Individually Quick Frozen, or IQF) and so **consumers** can easily pour only the required amount from a bag.

Fresh peas are brought to the fluidised bed freezer on a conveyer

The refrigerated air freezes the peas separately, so they do not clump together

Refrigerated air is blown upwards through the fluidised bed

Frozen peas are taken on a conveyer to be stored

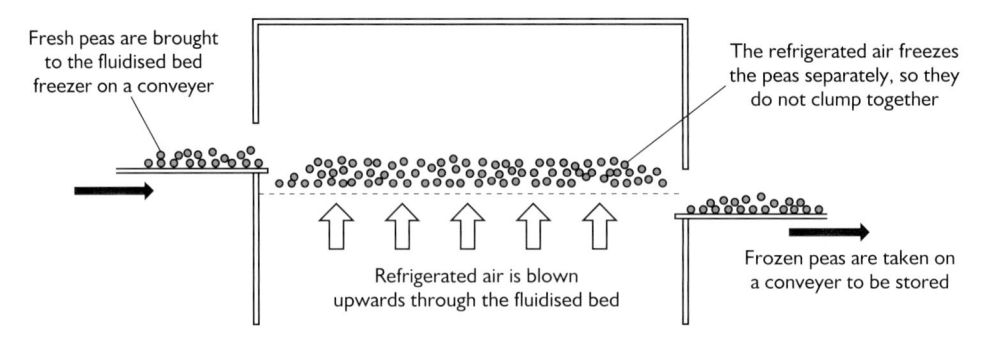

Diagram showing how peas are frozen in a fluidised bed freezer

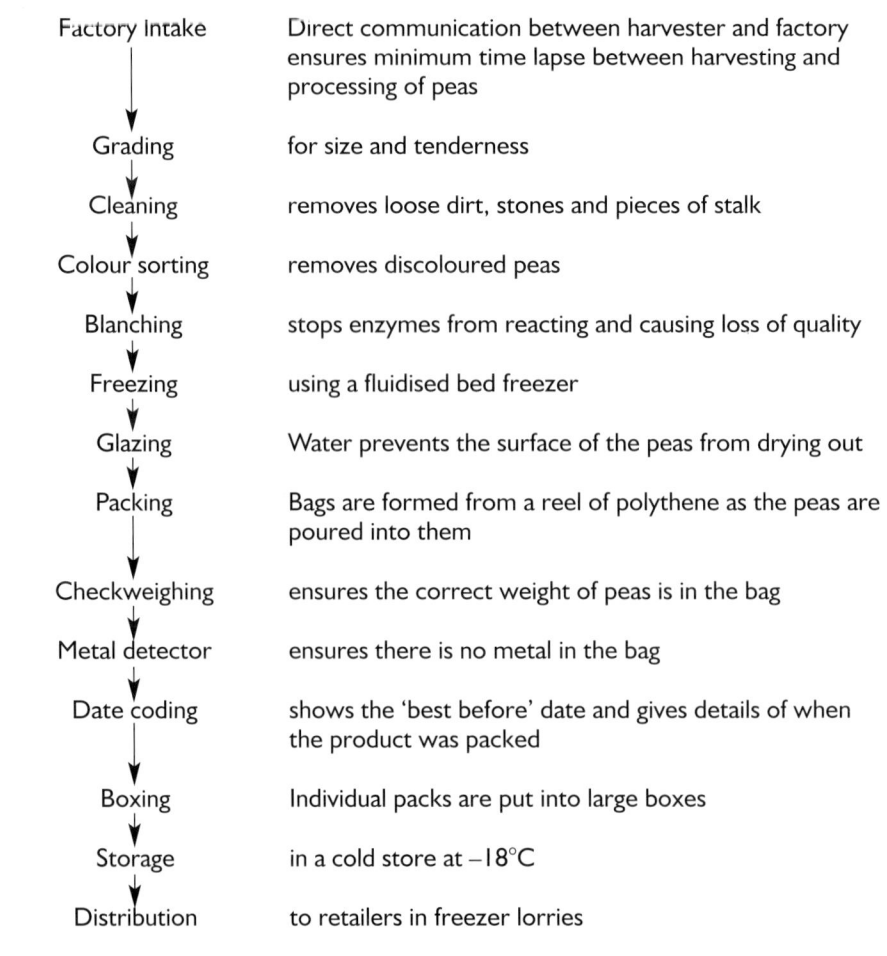

Factory Intake	Direct communication between harvester and factory ensures minimum time lapse between harvesting and processing of peas
Grading	for size and tenderness
Cleaning	removes loose dirt, stones and pieces of stalk
Colour sorting	removes discoloured peas
Blanching	stops enzymes from reacting and causing loss of quality
Freezing	using a fluidised bed freezer
Glazing	Water prevents the surface of the peas from drying out
Packing	Bags are formed from a reel of polythene as the peas are poured into them
Checkweighing	ensures the correct weight of peas is in the bag
Metal detector	ensures there is no metal in the bag
Date coding	shows the 'best before' date and gives details of when the product was packed
Boxing	Individual packs are put into large boxes
Storage	in a cold store at −18°C
Distribution	to retailers in freezer lorries

How frozen peas are produced using a fluidised bed freezer

4 A cryogenic freezer uses liquid gas as the freezing medium. It operates at very low temperatures and can be used for small delicate foods like soft fruits.

Shelf life in a domestic freezer is less than in an industrial cold store because of its small size. Every time the door is opened there is some fluctuation in the temperature inside the freezer. Storage life for foods is indicated by the 'star' (★) rating of the freezer. This depends upon the ability of the freezer to maintain a steady temperature of –18°C.

☆★★★ } Keep foods until best (freezer temperature must be
★★★ } before date –18°C or below)

The white star (☆) indicates that the freezer is suitable for freezing food, as well as for frozen storage.

Coursework checkpoint 1: *freezing*

1 Use a temperature probe to check the temperature inside a freezer at your school.
2 Monitor the temperature daily for a week and draw a graph to show temperature variation.
3 Suggest reasons for any variations that you find.

Coursework checkpoint 2: *freezing*

1 Try freezing a range of food ingredients, such as cabbage, sliced carrots, milk, whole tomatoes and cheese.
2 Record their textural characteristics when they are fresh, then put a small quantity of each into a bag and put it into the freezer for 24 hours. (Milk must be put into a container such as a plastic jar – DO NOT put a glass bottle into the freezer.)
3 Record the changes that you find to their **appearance**, then allow each to thaw and again note any changes from the original material. From your observations decide which materials are not suitable for freezing.

functional properties of food ingredients affect their selection and the way they are used in foods. For example:

- **sugar** is added to jam to give **taste** (sweetness) and to help preserve it
- butter or margarine are used for making **pastry**. Both would provide shortening, but the pastry would taste different in each case.
- whole **egg** is used as a **binder** and **glazing** agent, to make a food set, and to increase the **protein** content of a food
- **starch** and modified **starch** are widely used as **thickeners**.

Coursework checkpoint: *functional properties*

1 Bake a sponge cake, with some of your group using margarine and some using butter as an ingredient.
2 Compare the cakes for **appearance** and taste. Which cake do you prefer? What difference does using butter make to the price of producing the cake?

Understanding Industrial Practices: Food Technology © Nelson Thornes 2005

g

In your coursework project you will need to:

- produce and use a plan to show the deadlines for the design and manufacture of your product
- use a time plan to show how long each stage of manufacture will take
- work to realistic deadlines.

a **Gantt chart** can be used to plan a project, showing the tasks to be done and number of weeks available to do them. The project can be planned in the following way:

- List the tasks in the order in which they need to be started.
- Use a horizontal line to show how long each task will take.
- Plan the tasks which might overlap and which can be done at the same time.

Task	Weeks												
	1	2	3	4	5	6	7	8	9	10	11	12
1												
2												
3												
4												
5												
6												
7												

You can use a Gantt chart to plan your coursework project

Coursework checkpoint: *Gantt chart*

You can use a Gantt chart to help plan your next project.

- Find out the number of weeks available and the deadline for your project.
- Copy the layout of the chart shown above and list the tasks you have to do in order.
- Use a coloured horizontal line to estimate the number of weeks each task will take.
- Remember to plan which tasks you can do at the same time – for example you may be able to develop your **design brief**, undertake research and develop your **design specification** at the same time (concurrently).
- Use a different coloured horizontal line to show the actual time each task took. If you do this you will show where you had to make any changes to your **production planning**. Remember to record and explain any changes you make to the design or manufacture of your product resulting from problems in meeting your coursework deadline. This will enable you to explain how you could manufacture identical products in **high volume**.

a **gel** is a substance where molecules of liquid are trapped within a solid. This gives a product that is 'set', such as in jam and jellies. A gelling agent is needed to help form the gel. This will form a network of molecules that will trap the water molecules inside it. Gelatin, pectin and **starch** are examples of gelling agents, which can also be used as **thickeners** because they trap the water in the food.

Some **carbohydrates** known as gums can also be used to form gels in foods. Only a very small quantity of a gum is required to form a gel.

Different gums produce gels of different strength and **texture**. Gums can also be mixed together, so the **manufacturer** can create a wide variety of gels of different strength and texture in foods. Some 'pour-over' dessert sauces use gums as gelling agents.

genetically modified (GM) foods have undergone a technique to add, remove or alter an individual gene. This is done to bring about improved characteristics in the food. **Maize** and soya beans are among crops where GM strains have been produced, in order to make them resistant to herbicides, and to resist attack by some insect pests. This leads to higher yields of the crops. Both maize and soya are widely used as food ingredients.

GM tomatoes have also been produced. These have been adapted so that they are denser and drier then normal tomatoes. This makes them ideal for use in producing tomato purée. Vegetarian rennet, which can be used in cheese making, is made by adapting yeast cells.

GM foods are only approved for sale in the EU after extensive safety assessment has been completed. Currently, there is still great **consumer** resistance to the use of GM foods within the EU.

People who support GM products say they can help to eradicate world hunger problems. Opponents say that it is 'against nature' to alter genes in plants and animals.

glazing is a finishing **process** that is used to improve the **aesthetic** qualities of a number of foods, such as pies and pastries.

- An **egg** glaze added to **pastry** before baking will give a glossy, attractive golden-brown finish to the pastry. This is a result of the **browning** reaction that occurs during baking. Milk gives similar results, but the finish is lighter in **colour** and not glossy.
- A **sugar** solution can be brushed over products, such as hot-cross buns, immediately after they are removed from the oven. The water evaporates, leaving a slightly sticky, sweet topping to the buns.
- In industry, a gelatin-based glaze can be used, for example on some meat products, to provide a clear, glossy finish. Water is used to glaze some small frozen foods, such as prawns or peas, to prevent them from drying out while they are in frozen storage.

a **hazard** is anything that might affect **food safety** and has the potential to cause harm to the **consumer**. The hazard may be:
- biological, such as **pathogens** like Salmonella or E. coli which might cause food poisoning
- chemical, such as the presence in food of cleaning fluid left in a machine
- physical, such as the presence in food of foreign objects like bits of bone or fragments of metal from a machine.

hazard analysis means identifying all the potential **hazards** and risks involved in manufacturing and consuming food products. All risks to people, the environment and in manufacturing processes must be assessed. Every source of danger in the factory must be removed or identified to avoid industrial accidents. Staff must be given appropriate training and must be supplied with the necessary protective clothing and equipment. All risks to **consumers** must be eliminated or the consumer given the necessary information to control the risk.

As a result of hazard analysis, some factories are separated into **high risk** and **low risk areas**, in order to prevent food from becoming recontaminated once it has been processed. Workers in food factories are trained to work and handle food in a safe and hygienic manner.

> **Coursework checkpoint:** *hazard analysis*
>
> 1. List potential hazards that a manufacturer could identify in the production of:
>   - bread
>   - a chicken portion
>   - a veggie burger.
> 2. List the precautions needed to prevent cross-contamination between raw mince and cooked ham.

Hazard Analysis Critical Control Point (HACCP)

(pronounced hassup) is concerned with **food safety**, to make sure that the food cannot be harmful to the **consumer** in any way. It is an essential part of the **quality control (QC)** procedures used in food production. HACCP involves examining in detail every operation in the production process, to identify potential **hazards** that would affect the product. A hazard is considered 'critical' if its occurrence will affect the safety of the final product. The stage at which the hazard is dealt with is called a **critical control point (CCP)**. Procedures must be put in place to control the hazard at the CCP and a monitoring system used to make sure the control is effective.

To help you understand how HACCP works, look at Table 3 showing how foods are checked to ensure no pieces of metal (that might fall off machinery) are in the packets.

In your coursework project you will need to:

- take responsibility for recognising hazards to product safety in making and storing your product. Make sure any hazards are removed wherever possible.
- identify CCPs
- devise QC procedures to monitor CCPs
- take action on any unsatisfactory test results
- keep a record of test results to prove that your product is safe.

Processing step	Hazard	Control measures	Monitoring
The food (e.g. chicken nuggets) is sealed into the finished pack	If a tiny piece of metal has broken off a machine it might be inside a chicken nugget. It might harm someone who ate it. A piece of metal is a hazard that must be controlled and the metal detector is a CCP.	The packs of nuggets go past a metal detector. If there is any metal inside a pack, it will be rejected from the production line.	A QC technician will check at regular intervals that the metal detector is working properly. Any rejected packs of food will be checked to find out what has happened to them. All checks are recorded on a check sheet.

Table 3 How foods are checked for foreign metal objects

By carrying out this QC procedure, the **manufacturer** *knows* that no packs with a piece of metal in them can reach the consumer.

> **Coursework checkpoint:** *Hazard Analysis Critical Control Point (HACCP)*
>
> Record in your coursework folder the potential hazards in product safety in manufacturing your product. Identify the CCPs and the steps you have taken to make sure your product is safe.

health and safety (H&S) at work is the responsibility of both employers and employees. The Health and Safety at Work Act 1974 requires **manufacturers** to follow strict rules and regulations and to have a H&S system in place. They must undertake a **hazard analysis** and **risk assessment** of every situation to make the workplace as safe as possible. Employees are required to follow safety procedures in order to reduce risks when using materials, machinery and manufacturing processes.

Manufacturers are also required to ensure a product's safety so that no harm can come to the user or the environment. For example, if a food product causes illness to **consumers** the manufacturer may face prosecution.

In your coursework project you will need to:

- follow safety rules when developing and making products
- carry out safety checks on tools, equipment and machinery
- use **quality assurance (QA)** and **quality control (QC)** procedures to make sure that your product will be safe for your intended consumer.

Safety with people	Safety with materials	Safety with equipment
Tie hair back	Handle materials with care. Read and follow handling instructions.	Take care with knives
Do not wear open-toed shoes	Wear protective gloves when moving food into or out of the oven	Switch machines off after use
Wear protective clothing	Take care with hot liquids	Put tools away after use
Follow safety rules	Clean up spills	Leave equipment clean

Table 4 Some of the potential hazards found in a food factory and the safety procedures needed to avoid accidents

Coursework checkpoint: *health and safety (H&S)*
- Read the safety rules in your kitchen.
- Keep your work area tidy.
- Handle food materials and equipment with care.
- Check that guards are in position on machinery.
- Read instructions before using machinery.
- If you are not sure about something, then ask.

heat processing is the application of heat to foods in order to bring about changes. All heating processes may cause changes in the sensory and nutritional qualities of the food. Temperature and time are essential **critical control points (CCPs)** for heat processing. **Chilling** and **freezing**, which both involve the *removal* of heat from food, are also heat processing operations.

Reasons for heat processing include:

- stopping **enzymes** from taking part in chemical reactions, as in **blanching**
- the destruction of **micro-organisms** to make the food safe. Micro-organisms are destroyed by heat over a period of time. If the temperature is too low or the time too short, some micro-organisms may survive heat processing and the food may be unsafe to eat.
- to extend the food's **shelf-life** as in **pasteurisation** and **sterilisation** (canning and Ultra High Temperature (UHT)), chilling and freezing

- to make the food more tender and palatable for eating as in boiling, frying, roasting and baking
- to dry the food, for example in the manufacture of vegetable pieces for dried soup mixes, or the production of cornflakes.

> **Coursework checkpoint:** *heat processing*
>
> Different heat processing methods can change the taste of milk.
>
> 1 Taste samples of dried (reconstituted), pasteurised, sterilised and UHT milk.
>
> 2 Describe the differences in taste in each milk sample.

heat transfer describes the means by which heat travels into and through a food substance. When foods are heated, the heat is transferred by:
- conduction through a solid food like a joint of meat in an oven
- convection through a liquid food
- radiation through food under an electric grill.

The rate at which heat is transferred will depend upon:
- the structure of the food (fatty foods transfer heat faster than non-fatty foods)
- the temperature difference between the food and the source of heat (food heats up much faster in a hot oven than in a cool oven).

Heat is transferred through most foods by a mixture of conduction and convection. The food **manufacturer** needs to understand the composition and structure of the food being heated. If the food does not reach a high enough temperature for a sufficiently long time during processing it may be unsafe for the **consumer**. However, if it is over heated, or heated for too long, then its **quality** will be reduced.

a **high risk area** is a part of a factory that is totally separate from the rest of the factory. A pipeline through a wall brings processed food from the **low risk area** into the high risk area. The flow chart showing how fresh pasta is made on page 59 shows where a wall divides the factory into high and low risk areas. People working in the high risk area wear different coloured protective clothing to the rest of the factory. They must change every time they go in or out of the area.

Foods that are handled within the high risk area are *high risk foods*. These are foods that have been **heat processed** or cooked, so that **pathogens** and spoilage **bacteria** have been destroyed. **Micro-organisms**, including bacteria, could grow in these high risk foods. The food must therefore be packaged under conditions where there is no chance of it becoming recontaminated. High risk foods are normally kept chilled throughout their **shelf life**, so that if, by chance, any pathogens are present it is too cold for them to grow and multiply.

high volume production (mass production) is used for manufacturing large quantities of food products, such as bread, crisps or fish fingers, for stock or to order. A **continuous production** system is often used for high volume production. High volume production is a cost-effective method of making consistent products.

This kind of production is planned for ease-of-manufacture, using standardised ingredients, equipment and manufacturing processes. Quality control (QC) checks throughout manufacture ensure product consistency.

Many high volume production machines are monitored by sensors, so that they stop automatically if a fault occurs. For example, the machine dispensing mashed potato on to a ready-meal tray will stop if the potato runs out. Once the fault is corrected, the machine continues to function.

High Temperature Short Time (HTST) is a continuous process used when pasteurising milk. The milk must be heated to a temperature of 72°C for a minimum of 15 seconds, in order to be sure that harmful bacteria (pathogens) are destroyed. This time and temperature are a legal requirement. Although there is a suggestion that the 15-second time needs to be increased to respond to a possible link between milk and Crohn's disease, it is not yet law.

> **In your coursework project you will need to:**
> - develop a product that could be manufactured in quantity
> - choose the most suitable **method of production** for your product and give reasons for choosing it
> - use QC checks to manufacture a high **quality** product.

Diagram showing a section through part of a plate heat exchanger, used for pasteurising milk

hygiene in food handling includes all the precautions and procedures that are needed to:

a) prevent the food from becoming contaminated, by physical sources such as soil from vegetables, chemical sources such as cleaning products or biological sources such as bacteria and moulds that would be present on an unclean work top.

b) prevent any micro-organisms that may be present from growing and multiplying so that they become a health risk to the consumer, or cause the food to spoil.

c) ensure the health of people working with the food.

Hygienic practice, therefore, involves all the equipment and machinery used in food preparation, the way the food itself is handled and also the people using it. This hygiene practice should be applied in food preparation in a factory and in a domestic kitchen.

> **In your coursework project you will need to:**
> - follow class hygiene rules
> - work in a safe and hygienic manner when handling food materials
> - clean your equipment and tools as you finish using them.

A food factory operative wearing protective clothing

What to do	When to do it	Why you should do it
Wash your hands	Before you start food preparation. Between handling raw and cooked food. After handling waste food or rubbish. After visiting the toilet. After eating.	To prevent cross-contamination of food with micro-organisms, via your hands
Cover cuts and wounds with a waterproof dressing	Put on a clean dressing before you start to handle food. Dressings should be blue.	A dressing is needed to prevent the risk of contaminating the food. The blue colour makes it easy to see if it comes off. Food that might have become contaminated can then be destroyed.
Remove jewellery, including wristwatches	Before you start to handle food	Jewellery can harbour bacteria that could be transferred to the food. There is also a risk of gems or fastenings coming off and contaminating the food.
Wear protective clothing. This includes an apron (preferably a white coat that covers all the normal clothing), a hat and a hair net. In food factories, beards should also be covered with a snood. Sometimes special shoes may also be needed.	All protective clothing should be put on immediately before entering the food preparation area and removed immediately on leaving the area. It should be washed before it is worn again.	To prevent contamination of the food and keep your clothes clean. Hair covering prevents loose hair from falling into the food.

Table 5 Procedures for personal hygiene

What to do	When to do it	Why you should do it
Keep food covered, or put it away	Any time when you are not actually working with it	To prevent contamination
Use the correct storage temperature	Always	To make sure that micro-organisms cannot grow. To keep the eating quality of the food at its best.
Have separate storage areas for raw and cooked foods	Always. In industry these will be kept in separate areas; in the home, refrigerated raw foods should always be stored below cooked foods.	To avoid any chance of spillage of raw foods on to cooked foods
Dispose of any waste in bins that are emptied regularly	As soon as you have finished using the products	To prevent spillages and to make sure nothing is lying around to attract pests

Table 6 Procedures for food hygiene

What to do	When to do it	Why you should do it
Keep the working area clean	'Clean as you go' is the rule for food preparation	To prevent cross-contamination by bacteria and make sure nothing is lying around to encourage pests
Clear up any spillages on the floor	Immediately after they happen	To make sure the floor is safe for other people to walk on, and that nothing is lying around to encourage pests
Wash up tools and equipment you have used	As soon as possible after you finish using them	Prevents food from hardening on to tools and equipment. This could harbour bacteria.
Use different equipment for different foods. For example, chopping boards used for meat should be separate to those used for vegetables.	Whenever you prepare food	Prevents cross-contamination from one type of food to another

Table 7 Procedures for equipment and tools hygiene

Understanding Industrial Practices: Food Technology © Nelson Thornes 2005

In industry, machinery hygiene involves stopping the **production line** at regular intervals and cleaning everything – all machinery and the conveyors that the food travels on. Some machines must be taken to pieces to clean them, others are designed to be cleaned by having a suitable steriliser flushed through them, followed by rinsing with water. This method of cleaning machinery is known as cleaning in place (CIP). It is preferred in industry since it is much quicker and needs fewer people to carry it out.

> **Coursework checkpoint:** *hygiene*
>
> 1 Walk round your kitchen at home or in school.
>   - List areas and equipment that you think are unhygienic because they have been poorly designed.
>   - List areas and equipment that you think have not been cleaned properly.
>   - Discuss your findings with your teacher.
>
> 2 List and explain four hygiene points that you should carry out when working with food.

In your coursework project you will need to:

- understand and use industrial practices and **systems and control** when designing and making your product
- choose a suitable **method of production** so your product is cost-effective to manufacture
- understand the roles of key people (see page 89) such as clients, designers, **technologists**, manufacturers and consumers.

industrial practices are process-based activities that enable food manufacturers to make cost-effective products at a profit. These can include designing and manufacturing activities like **product development (PD)**, using a **design brief** to generate ideas, using computer-aided design/computer-aided manufacture (CAD/CAM) for production and using **quality control (QC)**.

The industrial practices used by manufacturers depend on the type of products they make and the **consumers** they are selling to. Examples include:

1 Design activities
- Market research – **tastes**, trends, **values issues**.
- Target market research – use a commercial approach.
- Product analysis – examine similar commercial products.
- Internet research – for ideas, ingredients or equipment.
- Develop a design brief.
- Use a **design specification** to generate and evaluate ideas.
- Use CAD **modelling**.
- Present ideas to the **clients/consumers** and use **feedback** to improve the design proposal.
- Develop a suitable production method.
- Design **quality** and safety into the product.
- Develop a **product specification** and a **manufacturing process specification**.

2 Manufacturing activities

- Use manufacturing process specifications.
- Work out the cost of factory production of the product.
- Plan production using **batch** or **high volume** methods.
- Use quality control.
- Use safe working practices.
- Test and evaluate against specifications.
- Evaluate potential sales of the product.
- Use feedback to suggest improvements.

Coursework checkpoint: *industrial practices*

○ Read the list of design and manufacturing activities listed on page 42 and above.

○ Identify which industrial practices you plan to use in your coursework project.

○ Check out the roles of key people (see page 89) involved in the production process.

Information and Communication Technology (ICT) has

revolutionised the way the food industry works, enabling companies to communicate information quickly, to source ingredients and to manufacture and sell on a global scale. ICT makes use of electronic and **computer systems**, which can:

1. Enable business partners to 'talk' to each other via electronic links such as:
   - Integrated Services Data Network (ISDN)
   - the Internet
   - Electronic Point of Sale (EPOS) tills.

2. Provide computer control such as:
   - computer-aided design (CAD)
   - computer-aided manufacture (CAM).

Electronic links can be used to:

- link business partners by e-mail or video conferencing
- import information from across the world
- source and handle data such as ordering stock
- send CAD information to **clients** for approval
- send a **product specification** to a distant production site
- develop in one location and manufacture in another (global manufacturing)
- enable **just in time** (JIT) manufacturing
- provide sales information through EPOS
- link retailers and **manufacturers**.

Coursework checkpoint: *Information and Communication Technology (ICT)*

1. The use of ICT has revolutionised food manufacturing, enabling research data, to be collected from different locations. Explore the possibility of collecting information in this way, using some of the following:

In your coursework project you will need to use:

- CAD to develop package and **label** designs
- CAD to produce an accurate **flow chart** of your manufacturing process
- computer software to present work, produce specification sheets and model costs
- software to simulate **production lines**.

Understanding Industrial Practices: Food Technology © Nelson Thornes 2005

- CD-ROMs or databases (to find out information about ingredients or products).
- E-mail (to share information with other students or to contact manufacturers).
- The Internet (to find out information about food materials, processes and products).
- Video conferencing (to share information with other students).

2 ICT systems enable the use of CAD for the development of food products. Investigate how you could use computer software to help you:
- edit research information
- scan ingredient information
- design a product specification sheet
- develop designs and colourways on screen for **packaging design**
- design a table or flow chart to plan the production of your product
- record your **product development (PD)** using a digital camera.

> **In your coursework project you will need to:**
> - make an ingredients list for your product, starting with the ingredient that your product contains the most of, and finishing with the one it contains the least of
> - use **Information and Communication Technology (ICT)** to update your ingredients list whenever you make a recipe change.

an **ingredients list** is found on the label of pre-packaged foods. Ingredients must be listed in weight order, starting with the greatest. Foods that have just one ingredient, e.g. tea or cornflour, are excluded from this requirement. The percentage of any ingredient used to help describe the food must be given. For example, a steak and kidney pie must include the percentage of steak and the percentage of kidney it contains and a tin of mushroom soup must state the percentage of mushrooms it contains. If a food is described as 'flavoured', e.g. 'meat flavoured' or 'banana flavoured', then it includes just flavouring, not the ingredient itself.

Tomato & Brown Lentil soup

INGREDIENTS: Water, Brown Lentils (23% Cooked), Carrots, Onions, Potatoes, Swede, Concentrated Tomato Paste (3%), Tomatoes (2.5%), Peas, Modified Cornflour, Salt, Yeast Extract, Honey, Soy Sauce, Garlic Puree, Paprika, Dried Parsley, Black Pepper Extract.

CONTAINS: SOYA, WHEAT, GLUTEN.

Roast Chicken FLAVOUR CRISPS

ROAST CHICKEN FLAVOUR CRISPS INGREDIENTS: Potatoes, vegetable oil, roast chicken flavour [flavouring, flavour enhancers (monosodium glutamate, disodium 5'-ribonucleotide), colour (paprika extract), hydrolysed soy protein], salt.
✓ Suitable for vegetarians ✓ Suitable for coeliacs
✓ No artificial colours

Two examples of food ingredient lists

> **Coursework checkpoint:** *ingredients list*
> - Check the ingredients shown on the packaging of foods such as salad cream, a Victoria sponge cake and ice-cream.
> - List the ingredients and try to work out why each one has been included in the product.

the **International Standards Organisation (ISO)** is a body that has drawn up standard procedures that companies should follow to show they are conforming to 'good practice' in their operations. For the food industry the main standards are numbers ISO 9001 and ISO 9002. Food factories follow one of these standards to demonstrate they are using a suitable **quality system**.

Many UK food **manufacturers** have been inspected and awarded an ISO certificate. ISO registered food manufacturers generally buy food materials from ISO registered suppliers to ensure a high **quality** supply. This system shows the **client** (usually the major supermarkets) that the manufacturer's quality system reaches the approved level.

irradiation is a food preservation method that can be used to destroy **micro-organisms**. It can also be used to prevent **enzymes** helping chemical reactions to occur within the food. Irradiated potatoes will not sprout when they are stored for long periods and irradiated fruits, such as strawberries, will not go soft once they are picked. However, widespread **consumer** resistance means that little irradiated food is sold in the UK.

j

just in time (JIT) manufacturing makes use of Information and Communication Technology (ICT) to help plan the ordering of materials. This is a complex **system** that requires careful planning between a **manufacturer** and its suppliers.

In JIT manufacturing goods arrive at a food factory just in time for production. There is no time for **quality control (QC)** tests when they arrive so the manufacturer has to be certain that the supplier will always send goods that match the buying **specification**. This is often achieved when the manufacturer and supplier have been awarded an International Standards Organisation (ISO) certificate.

JIT has a number of advantages for the manufacturer. It:

- reduces the need for stockpiles of **raw materials**, waiting to be used
- reduces the space needed for keeping raw materials in stock
- reduces the levels of finished goods put into stock, waiting to be sold
- cuts the costs of tying up money in stock.

In your coursework project you will need to:
- produce and use a detailed work schedule that specifies the materials you will use
- use a time plan to set deadlines for the different stages of manufacture.

l

a **label** must be placed on pre-packaged foods to give information about the food. The label can be written separately and stuck on to the package or placed around it as a sleeve. Alternatively, the information can be written directly on to the **packaging material**, for example, on drinks cans or biscuit packets. In this case it is still referred to as a 'label'.

Some information about the food must be given by law. This includes:

- the name of the food
- the list of ingredients
- the 'best before' or 'use by' date, depending on **shelf life**

In your coursework project you will need to:
- use **computer-aided design (CAD)** to design a label for your product.

- any special storage instructions. For example, 'After opening, keep refrigerated for up to 3 months. Do not freeze' may be written on a jar of mayonnaise.
- name and address of the company responsible for the product. This will be the **manufacturer** for a **brand** name product or a supermarket for an **own-label** product, or sometimes the importer for a foreign product.
- instructions for use, if these are necessary. If other ingredients are needed to make the product this should be clearly stated. For example, a cake mix might have the words, 'add **eggs**' written on the packet.
- country of origin of the food, if this is necessary so as not to mislead the customer. For example, pineapple pieces could be marked as 'product of the Philippines' or as 'product of Thailand'.
- nett weight of product. By law, this information is necessary on most foods.

Food product labels

The label may also contain a picture of the product. This must be a fair representation of the product. For example:

- if a frozen gateau has four cherries on top it must not be shown in the picture with eight cherries on top
- if the food, such as a sauce, is going to be part of a meal, a picture showing a plate of food with the sauce included must have the words 'serving suggestion' beside it. **Consumers** must not think that *everything* in the picture is in the packet.

Many manufacturers choose to give more information than is required by law. This may include:

- nutritional information
- 'recipe suggestions' – these are to encourage consumers to try using their products
- price.

Coursework checkpoint: *label*

Examine the labels from a range of different food products. Analyse the labels and explain how you think each label helps to sell the food product.

legislation requires that everyone involved in the production and sale of food has to conform to a number of complex laws. These ensure that **consumers** receive only food that is safe to eat and that is of satisfactory quality. Some topics covered by legislation include:

- food safety
- food hygiene
- the temperature that foods are kept at
- food labelling
- use of **preservatives**.

Environmental concerns are also addressed by legislation, including:

- pesticides in food
- disposal of waste products, such as animal waste and waste oil from crisp **manufacturers**
- disposal and recycling of **packaging materials**.

Coursework checkpoint: *legislation*

- Collect examples of packaging and **labels** used on a range of products similar to your own.
- Design similar labelling for your own product.

lifestyle marketing is where **manufacturers** and retailers target potential **consumers** and match their needs with food products. **Market research** is carried out to identify the buying behaviour, **taste** and lifestyle of the potential consumers. This establishes the amount of money they have to spend, their age group and which types of food products they like to buy. New food products can then be developed to match the customer needs. A **marketing** plan is developed to promote the new product.

In your coursework project you will need to:

- check that your product will be safe for your intended consumer.

a **low risk area** is the part of a factory where foods undergo preparation and processing. The processing destroys any **pathogens** in the food. The food will not leave the factory before it has been processed and so it presents a low risk to **consumer** health. The **flow chart** showing how fresh pasta is made on page 59 shows where a wall divides the factory into high and low risk areas. *After* the food has been processed it passes into the **high risk area** of the factory where very stringent precautions are in place to prevent recontamination occurring. Foods must never leave the low risk area until staff are sure that processing has been satisfactorily completed. People working in the low risk area do not need to change their protective clothing every time they go into or out of their area.

Foods that offer minimal risk to the consumer, because pathogens do not grow in them, are known as low risk foods. These include products such as **sugar**, frozen vegetables and bread.

m

maize is a cereal, often known simply as 'corn'. Maize is sold as 'corn-on-the-cob' and as 'sweetcorn'. It is a valuable source of vegetable oil. **Starch** is extracted from maize and sold as cornflour.

Maize is used as an ingredient in **secondary foods** such as breakfast cereals and popcorn. For food **manufacturers** maize starch is an important **thickener**. Many **modified starches** are made from maize starch for use in foods such as frozen pies, canned foods and sauces.

a **manufacturing process specification** must be written once a development **prototype** has successfully met the **design specification**. It must include all the detailed information that is needed to manufacture the product so that it will meet the **product specification**. For example, if a factory is making fresh, pre-packed fruit salad, the manufacturing process specification might include:

- the formulation (recipe) for the product
- storage information for all the fruits (what temperature they should be stored at and how long each may be kept)
- how each fruit should be cleaned, if necessary
- how each fruit should be peeled, if necessary
- how each fruit should undergo **size reduction** (e.g. slicing kiwi fruit – include the thickness of the slices; dicing melons – include the size of the dice)
- how the fruit should be stored and transported once it has been cut up
- how many pieces of each fruit should be placed in the plastic tray
- what the nett weight of the product should be. (The nett weight is the weight of the product. It is the total product weight minus the weight of the tray.)
- how the tray should be sealed
- how the pre-printed **label** should be attached to the tray
- the **shelf life** of the product. (The 'use by' date and any 'sell by'

date required by the retailer must be printed on to the label, once the product is packed.)
- how the packaged product should be stored (in a refrigerator – give the temperature)
- the maximum time the product can be stored before being sent out to the retailer.

A manufacturing process specification should also include:
- a **flow chart**, showing **critical control points (CCPs)** and other points where **quality control (QC) testing** must take place
- details of QC tests (including what checks are needed and the frequency with which they must be carried out). Acceptable test results will also be given, with information on what to do if the results are not acceptable.

market research is carried out by **manufacturers** to identify the buying behaviour, taste and lifestyle of potential **consumers**. A market research report can establish the size of the **target market group**, the product to be developed, product price ranges and the competition from products from other manufacturers.

1 Primary market research can be collected through:
   - a shop report to identify product information and new ideas
   - **product analysis** of similar products to find out about ingredients and packaging, manufacturing processes, **quality** and value for money
   - questionnaires to ask intended users about the products they buy and their likes and dislikes
   - industrial visits
   - visits to food shows
   - interviews with experts such as chefs, teachers, other adults.

A market research report can provide useful information about the food product to be developed, the intended target market group, eating trends, new ideas, **packaging design** details and the product price range. A report can involve:
- going into stores and restaurants to look for ideas, trends and themes
- watching television programmes about food-related topics
- going to specialist food shops, craft fairs and museums to look for ideas about food in relation to society.

Buying behaviour can establish the profile of a potential target market group, such as:
- the amount of money they have to spend
- their age group
- their taste and personality, influenced by nationality, lifestyle, family group, **brand** loyalty, which products they like to buy, e.g. Coca-cola; Mars Bars.

2 Secondary market research can be collected from existing information in:
   - magazines and newspapers
   - textbooks
   - TV programmes
   - CD-ROMs and databases
   - the Internet.

In your coursework project you will need to:

- take account of a range of consumers
- use cultural, social and environmental influences when developing your product ideas
- use the influence of traditional foods and the work of other manufacturers when developing ingredient and **flavour** ideas
- be flexible in the way that you respond to new ideas and new opportunities.

Coursework checkpoint: *market research*

1 Use market research techniques to find out ingredients and flavour trends for your intended product. You can do this by undertaking a shop report, which can involve visiting supermarkets, looking for ideas.
   - Decide which supermarkets you will visit.
   - Decide what information you need to find out.
   - Ask permission from the manager, if necessary, explaining why you're doing a shop report.

2 Make sketches and notes on products about:
   - ingredients used
   - **packaging materials** and design
   - alternative products available (low fat; reduced salt; organic)
   - sizes (nett weights) that the product is sold in
   - price ranges.

3 Compare your shop report with that of another student who aims to develop a similar food product to you.

4 Use the information you have collected to give you ideas about ingredients, packaging and eating trends.

5 Try to spot new trends that you could incorporate into your own product.

In your coursework project you will need to:

- take account of a range of consumers and their nutritional needs
- use cultural and social influences when developing your design ideas
- use the influence of traditional foods and the work of other food developers when developing ideas for your food product
- be flexible in the way that you respond to new ideas and new opportunities.

---

marketing involves developing a marketing plan for a product, so that it sells well to the **target market group**. It involves developing a competitive edge through providing reliable, high **quality** products at a price **consumers** can afford, combined with the image they want the product to give them. This is sometimes called **lifestyle marketing**.

1 A successful marketing plan uses **market research** to find out about:
   - user needs
   - consumer demand
   - the age, income and location of the market
   - the size of the market
   - the product type consumers want
   - the price range **clients** (customers) will pay
   - trends affecting the market
   - competitors' products and marketing style
   - the timescale to sell into the market.

2 A marketing plan can involve the advertising and promotion of **brands** through retailers, newspapers and magazines, TV, radio and the Internet.

Recent marketing trends include:
   - the use of cartoon characters to promote products, e.g. 'Bugs bunny' on chicken nuggets and 'Wallace and Gromit' on cheese
   - using 'storyline' adverts to promote products on television, e.g. Gold Blend coffee; Yakult.

Coursework checkpoint: *marketing*

Collect food product advertisements from magazines and try to identify the target market group the product is aimed at.

- Is a particular product type aimed at a specific age group?
- Is the product advertised in other media such as on TV, on street hoardings?
- Does the advertisement try to promote an image about the product?
- Is the product aimed at a particular lifestyle?
- Where does your product fit in with image and lifestyle marketing?

mechanical processing includes operations such as mixing dry ingredients and size reduction. During mechanical processing the food undergoes physical changes, but no chemical changes. For example,

1. If dry ingredients for a powdered soup are mixed, it would still be possible to separate the mixture back into its original components. They have been physically mixed, but are not chemically bound together.

2. If a carrot is cut into slices, it has undergone physical change, but each slice still has the same percentage chemical composition and nutritional value as the whole carrot.

metering is the term used when liquid or powdered ingredients, used to manufacture a product, are measured out either continuously or into a batch mixer. The *rate* at which a metered ingredient is added to the product mix is controlled, so that the correct proportion of each ingredient is always present. For example, batter being used to coat fish fingers will be pumped on to the production line at a given rate, to ensure that there is always enough batter to coat the fish.

a **method of production** (production system, manufacturing system, method of manufacture, scale of production) is decided by the type of food and the level of demand for it. Many foods have a peak seasonal demand, such as mince pies at Christmas or prepared salads in the summer, so the scale of production may vary throughout the year.

Methods of production can include:

- one-off (custom made)
- batch production for stock or order
- high volume (mass production) using continuous production (continuous flow) for very high demand products.

micro-organisms is the collective name for bacteria, yeast and moulds. They are single-celled, living organisms that can only be viewed under a microscope. Micro-organisms are so small that millions of them could fit on to a pinhead. They exist widely in the environment and in food materials. Some micro-organisms are used in food production (for example, yeast in bread making and bacteria in yoghurt production). Many micro-organisms cause problems either by spoiling the food (making it go 'off') or by making it unsafe to eat (if large numbers of harmful bacteria (pathogens) are present).

microwaveable foods are produced by many manufacturers to meet a high consumer demand for meals that are quick and easy to prepare. Many foods are suitable for microwave cooking, except for those where a crisp texture is required. For example, foods containing pastry or a crispy batter tend to go 'soggy' when cooked in the microwave. Very thick pieces of food, such as joints of meat, are also not suitable for microwave cooking as the microwaves cannot penetrate the food far enough to cook it.

In your coursework project you will need to:

- design a product that could be manufactured in quantity
- choose the most suitable method of production for your food and give reasons for choosing it
- understand what is meant by one-off, batch, high volume and continuous production
- give examples of foods produced by each method of production
- explain the advantages and disadvantages of each method of production
- understand how **quality assurance (QA)** systems and **quality control (QC)** techniques are used to manufacture high **quality** products.

Understanding Industrial Practices: Food Technology © Nelson Thornes 2005

Microwaveable foods can cause problems for manufacturers because different food materials heat up at different rates. This can lead to 'hot spots' and 'cold spots' in the cooked food. Microwaveable **packaging materials** such as plastic dishes can be designed to help even out the heating effect. Cooking instructions on the food packs often state that the food should be stirred halfway through cooking. Standing time also helps to even out the heat distribution within the food. Microwaved foods should have reached a temperature of at least 75°C during cooking to ensure **food safety**.

> **Coursework checkpoint:** *microwaveable foods*
>
> 1 Following the cooking instructions, prepare a ready-meal, such as macaroni cheese, which is made to be heated in a conventional oven. Also prepare macaroni cheese which is made to be heated in a microwave.
>
> 2 Describe differences in the **appearance** and **taste** of the cooked products.
>
> 3 List the advantages and disadvantages of using the microwave oven, compared to the conventional oven.

minerals are the chemical elements other than carbon, hydrogen, oxygen and nitrogen that are needed in the body. Calcium, iron and sodium are included among the major minerals required. Fluorine is needed only in very small amounts and is known as a trace element.

Mineral	Main uses of the mineral in the human body	Common foods which are good sources of the mineral
Calcium	For bones and teeth	Milk and cheese; bread
Iron	For the formation of haemoglobin found in red blood cells	Liver; plain chocolate; wholemeal bread; cornflakes and other breakfast cereals with added minerals
Sodium	For maintaining the fluid content of the body. High levels of salt intake are associated with high blood pressure which can bring on heart disease and strokes.	Most foods contain some sodium in the form of salt. Salt is often added to foods during cooking at home or at the table. Many manufacturers are introducing 'low salt' alternatives to their standard products, e.g. soups and baked beans, to help consumers cut down their salt intake.
Fluorine	For hardening tooth enamel and preventing tooth decay	Fish and tea. Many local authorities add fluorine to the drinking water supply.

Table 8 Why these minerals are needed and some foods that they can be found in

In your coursework project you will need to:

- understand that combining materials creates more useful properties
- use mixing processes suitable for your food product.

mixing is the **unit operation** used to blend a number of ingredients together. Nearly all foods contain at least two ingredients and some may contain more than a dozen. The method used in mixing will depend upon the nature of the ingredients.

- Liquids are easily mixed, provided they are miscible (mix easily like milk and water, for example). The stirring action must produce **turbulence** in the liquids to ensure proper mixing. Stirring with a spoon then reversing the stirring direction has the same effect in the domestic kitchen.
- Immiscible liquids (those that separate out from one another when they are left to stand), such as water and oil, need an **emulsifier** as well as a turbulent mixing action in order to make them blend together and not separate out.

- Doughs and pastes have a high viscosity (they are very thick and stiff). This means they are difficult to mix. An electric mixer with a strong motor and strong mixer blades is needed. A dough hook can be used to mix dough. This reaches into every part of the mixer bowl and ensures that every part of the ingredients is brought into the mix.
- Powders and small particles of dried vegetables, for example, are fairly easy to mix, as they are all similar in size. A tumble mixer can be used to mix the ingredients for a flavourings **pre-mix** or a powder dessert mix. A tumble mixer resembles a box on a stand. It can be half filled with ingredients. The mixer then revolves and tumbles the ingredients together.
- Where there is a large difference in the particle size of the different ingredients, such as in a dry soup mix with croutons, it is very difficult to get a satisfactory blending of all the ingredients. In this kind of mix it is more usual to mix the similar sized ingredients together first. The mix is then carried along a conveyor system and the larger ingredients are 'dribbled' into it as it moves to the packaging machines.

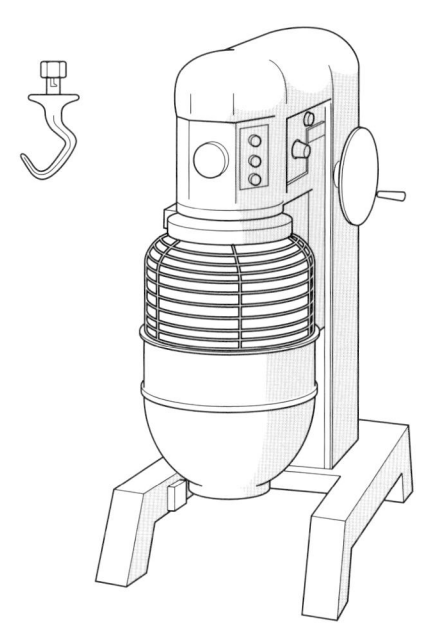

Diagram showing a dough hook and a mixer suitable for small-scale commercial dough mixing. Note the safety guard around the mixing bowl. The mixer will not work unless this is in place. This ensures that operatives cannot catch their fingers on the moving parts.

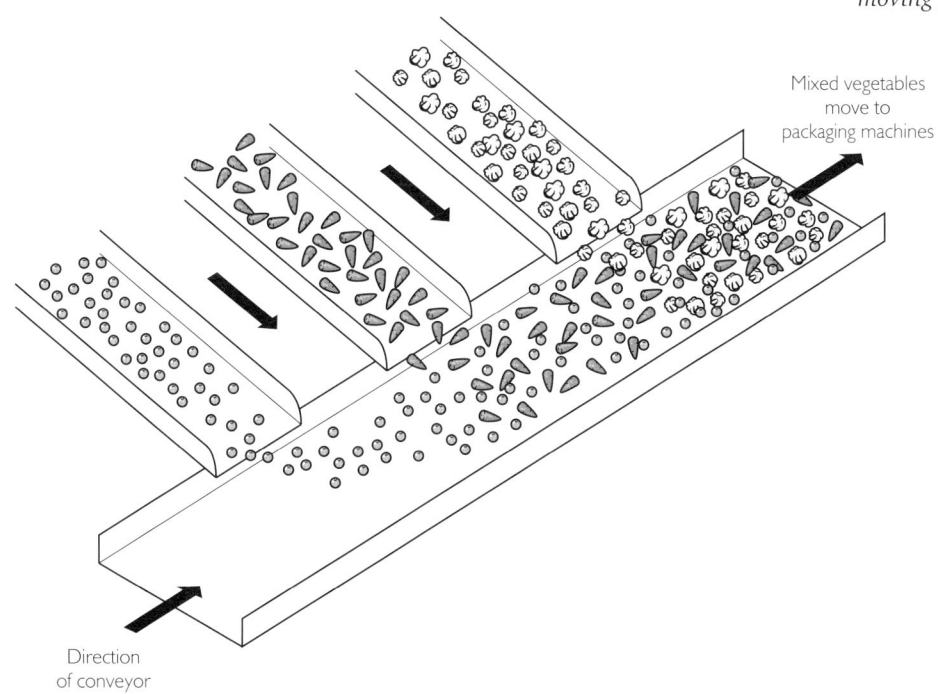

Diagram to show how a mixed vegetable product can be blended on a conveyor

- Mixing a very small amount of one ingredient (a minor ingredient) into a large batch is also a problem, as it is difficult to be sure that the ingredient will be evenly distributed. This problem may occur with **additives**, for example. It can be solved by using a pre-mix. For example, the salt and **flavour** ingredients used on crisps are pre-mixed, and it is the pre-mix that is used to coat the crisps.

modelling can be used to help develop and communicate ideas and design proposals for products and also for packaging. **Computer-aided design (CAD)** can be used to create 2D or 3D 'virtual' products on screen. It can also be used to design the most suitable layout of machinery in a factory.

modified starch refers to starch that has been altered or modified in some way, so that it can more easily perform a specific function in food manufacture. Modified starches are sometimes referred to as 'smart foods'.

There are several ways that starch can be modified. This means that when 'modified starch' is listed as a food ingredient it is not always the same product. Examples of modified starches include the following:

1. Pregelatinised starch forms a **gel** when it is added to water or milk without being heated. It is used in making instant desserts.

2. Freeze-thaw-stable starch is used in frozen foods. It prevents water from being released in the product when it is frozen (for example from gravy in a meat pie). This makes sure that the **taste** and **texture** of the food is the same before and after **freezing**.

3. Modified starch is used where some thickening of the product is needed in canned foods. The starch will not break down and become runny during the high temperatures used in **canning**.

n

non-starch polysaccharides (NSPs) are carbohydrates and form 'dietary fibre'. Dietary fibre is not a nutrient, but it is needed to maintain good health as it assists bowel action and helps to prevent cancer of the colon. Low dietary fibre intake is also thought to be associated with heart disease and diabetes. The outer (bran) layers of cereals (found in whole grain or wholemeal foods), vegetables and some fruits are good sources of dietary fibre.

nutritional information is supplied on the **labels** of most pre-packaged foods. The style in which it is presented is controlled by law. All nutritional values must be given per 100g of food and per serving, where that is relevant.

1. The *minimum* information a **manufacturer** may declare includes the following:
   - Four nutritional values: for energy, **protein**, **fat** and **carbohydrate**.
   - A manufacturer may not state a nutritional value just for protein, for example. Values for all four nutrients must be given. The left hand column in Table 9 shows how one manufacturer presented four nutritional values for tinned pineapple.

In your coursework project you will need to:

- understand the relationship between the properties of food materials and manufacturing processes, so that you make the best use of materials
- understand that food materials can be combined and processed to create more useful properties
- make sure that the properties of your food products are suitable for the **target market group**.

2 A manufacturer can also declare the following extra information:
- Four extra nutritional values: for **sugars** within the carbohydrates; for saturated fats within fats; for dietary fibre and for sodium.
- A manufacturer may not select and state *one* of these extra nutritional values, such as for dietary fibre. All four values must be declared, or none of them. The middle column in Table 9 shows how one manufacturer presented four extra nutritional values for crisps.

A manufacturer can also declare the **vitamins** present in food, provided that the amount present is at least 15% of the **Recommended Daily Amount (RDA)**.
- The food label must state the proportion of the RDA present, so that **consumers** can judge for themselves whether the food is a good source of the vitamins and provides value for money. The right hand column in Table 9 shows how one manufacturer presented the vitamins present in Marmite™.

	Tinned pineapple (values per 100g serving)	Crisps (values per 25g packet)	Marmite™ (values per 4g serving)
Energy	85kcal	131kcal	9kcal
Protein	0.4g	1.6g	1.5g
Carbohydrates (of which sugars)	20.0g	12.5g 0.5g	0.8g trace
Fat (of which saturates)	0.1g	8.3g 3.8g	trace trace
Dietary fibre		1.0g	0.1g
Sodium		0.2g	0.2g
Thiamin			0.23mg (16.5% RDA)
Riboflavin			0.28mg (17.5% RDA)
Niacin			6.4mg (35.6% RDA)
Folic acid			100.0µg (50.0% RDA)
Vitamin B12			0.6µg (60.0% RDA)

Table 9 Examples of nutritional information on food labels

o

one-off is a term used to describe **custom made** products.

organic foods are made using organically grown crops, organically raised animals, or organic fish. Organic farms are inspected and licensed every year to ensure they follow strict standards. The **consumer** market in organic foods is rising because of health and environmental concerns about the possible damage caused by using artificial fertilisers and pesticides. Organic foods are more expensive than conventionally produced foods because production is more labour intensive. Also, yields are lower, so the grower must receive a higher price or they would go out of business.

organoleptic describes the qualities of food that are appreciated by the **consumer's** senses of sight, smell and **taste**. **Aesthetic** appeal, **colour**, **aroma**, **flavour**, taste and **texture** are all organoleptic qualities.

own-label products are developed by a **manufacturer** in collaboration with a supermarket chain and are manufactured only for that supermarket. Supermarkets use own-label products to project their image and promote customer loyalty.

p

packaging design is important in the **marketing** of food. The food **manufacturer** decides which **packaging materials** are suitable for the product and for the manufacturing process. The manufacturer employs a specialist design company whose job is to produce a packaging design that will help to sell the product.

The designer works with the product and its **target market group** in mind. The packaging design needs to give the appropriate 'image' to the product. For example, glass is much heavier than plastic, but it can give a shinier, 'classier' effect for an expensive ready-made sauce product, but a plastic container might be used for a cheaper sauce.

The packaging designer needs to think about:

- the shape of the packaging. For example, the Coca Cola bottle has a very distinctive shape.
- the use of **colour**. Luxury items tend to use gold, silver and red. Low-price range products often have a white background and use very little colour.
- a picture of the product, either on its own or as a 'serving suggestion' to show how attractive it might look when it is served.
- the font type and size. This can highlight particular features of the packaging design.
- ensuring all legally required information can be easily seen by the **consumer**.

A range of packaging designs

packaging materials for foods include glass (bottles and jars), metal (cans and pouches), paper (bags and boxes) and plastics. Plastic is the most common packaging material as it can be used in many different forms, such as containers for ice-cream, bottles, trays for meat or ready-meals and film for bags and lids.

- Plastic film is supplied to a food factory on a reel (like kitchen paper, only the reels are much larger).
- The reel of film is lined up on the packaging machine. It may be used to form sealed lids over food containers immediately after the food is placed into them. Alternatively, plastic bags can be formed just as the food is placed into them.
- Food packaging lines run at very high speed and are very efficient.

Manufacturers need to consider cost when selecting packaging materials. The cost of the packaging must be covered in the price charged for the product. Manufacturers also have a legal obligation to reduce waste and ensure a high amount of packaging materials can be recycled. The packaging material must also fulfil some important functions:

1. To make the food easy for the **consumer** to handle and to use. The packaging material must:
   - weigh as little as possible
   - be strong enough not to burst or tear when the food package is handled
   - be properly sealed
   - be available in pack sizes that are convenient for the consumer
   - be easy to open.

2. To make sure that the food is kept preserved for the length of its **shelf life**.
   - Some packaging materials have an essential role in making sure food will not spoil. For example canned foods are **heat processed** after the food is filled into the metal can. The can prevents any recontamination by **micro-organisms** occurring.
3. To protect the food. The packaging materials must keep the food:
   - clean and hygenic while packs are being handled
   - free from attack by insects or other pests
   - free from being tainted by non-food products. Foods such as **flour** and tea very quickly pick up odours from soap powders and cleaning products. In the supermarket cleaning products are kept well away from tea and flour.
4. To supply consumers with all the information they need. This is provided on the **label**.

pasteurisation is a mild heat treatment for food using temperatures below 100°C. It is designed to destroy **pathogens** and to make sure that the food is safe for eating. It will not destroy *all* the **micro-organisms** that might cause the food to spoil, and so the product **shelf life** will not be as long as for foods that have undergone a **sterilisation** process. Because the heat treatment is only mild, pasteurised foods are considered to be 'fresh'. Pasteurised foods are often stored in a fridge to help extend their shelf life (for example, milk and fresh pasta).

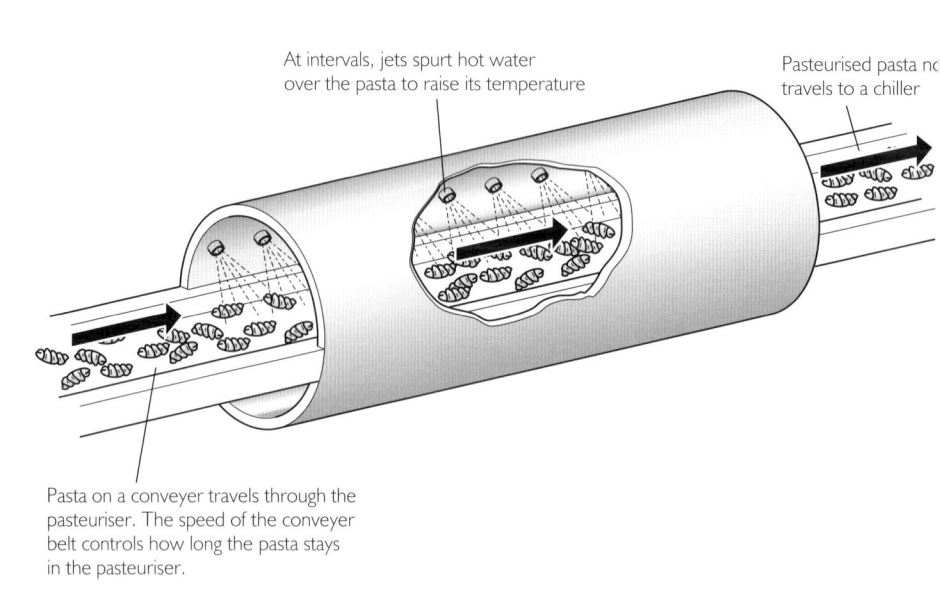

Pasta being pasteurised in a tunnel pasteuriser

Semolina (a coarse type of flour) metered out into the mixer → Mixing

Liquid egg metered out into the mixer → Mixing

Water metered out into the mixer → Mixing

Low risk area of the factory

- **Mixing**: The ingredients are mixed and kneaded to form a stiff dough
- **Extrusion**: The dough is forced out of the mixer through a die head (a metal block with holes through it). The design of the holes determines the shape of the pasta.
- **Cutting**: A rotating knife cuts the pasta into lengths as it leaves the die head. If the knife rotates fast the pasta will be short, if it rotates slowly the pasta will be long, e.g. spaghetti.
- **Pasteurisation**: The cut pasta falls on to a moving conveyor that moves through a tunnel pasteuriser. Jets of hot water mixed with steam heat the pasta to over 90°C as it travels through the tunnel. Pasteurisation time is controlled by the speed of the conveyor.
- **Chilling**: The conveyor with the pasta on it now enters a spiral chiller to be cooled to below 5°C.

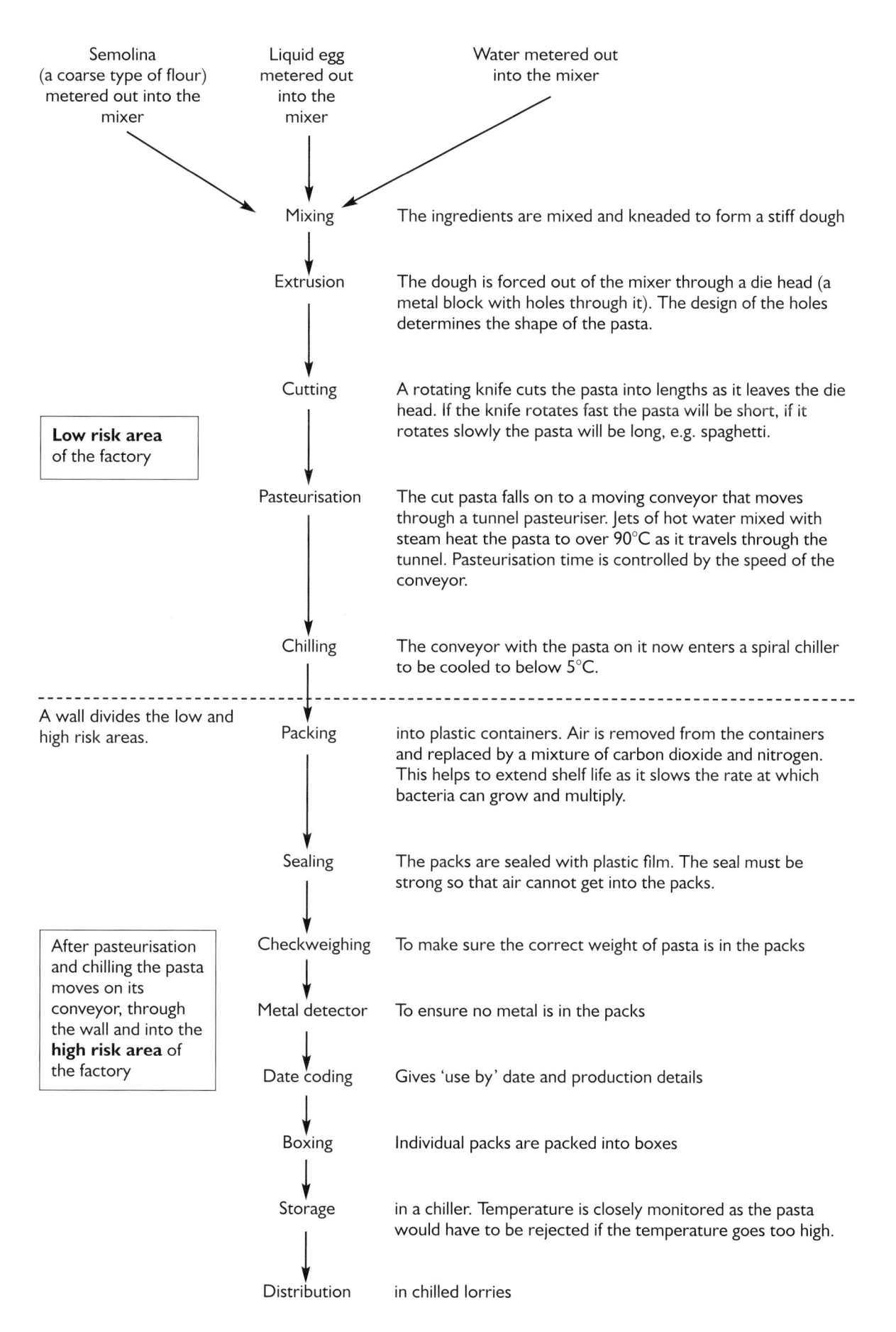

A wall divides the low and high risk areas.

- **Packing**: into plastic containers. Air is removed from the containers and replaced by a mixture of carbon dioxide and nitrogen. This helps to extend shelf life as it slows the rate at which bacteria can grow and multiply.
- **Sealing**: The packs are sealed with plastic film. The seal must be strong so that air cannot get into the packs.
- **Checkweighing**: To make sure the correct weight of pasta is in the packs
- **Metal detector**: To ensure no metal is in the packs
- **Date coding**: Gives 'use by' date and production details
- **Boxing**: Individual packs are packed into boxes
- **Storage**: in a chiller. Temperature is closely monitored as the pasta would have to be rejected if the temperature goes too high.
- **Distribution**: in chilled lorries

After pasteurisation and chilling the pasta moves on its conveyor, through the wall and into the **high risk area** of the factory

How fresh pasta is produced using pasteurisation

pastry is used to enclose other food substances so that they are convenient to eat. The main ingredient of pastry is wheat **flour** so the pastry also adds bulk to the food. The pastry has a different **texture** to the filling, so that eating the food is more enjoyable.

In industry the pastry ingredients are usually mixed using an 'all-in-one' method as this requires less labour. A batch of pastry mix may weigh over 100kg. Once it has been mixed the pastry is tipped into a feed hopper at the end of the **production line** where it is needed. It is then passed along the production line through several pairs of rollers. The gap between each pair of rollers gets smaller, so that the pastry is gradually reduced to the thinness required.

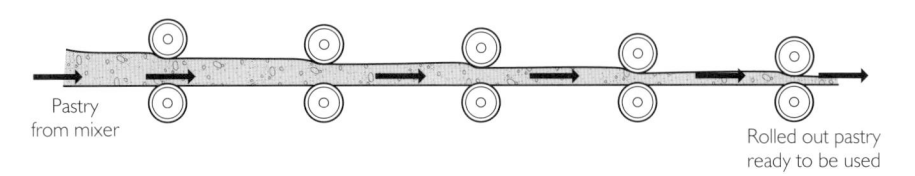

Pastry being reduced in thickness as it passes through sets of rollers

Type of pastry	Shortcrust	Puff	Filo
Main ingredients	Flour, fat and a little water	Flour, high level of fat, little water	Flour with high level of protein, fat and water
Working characteristics	'Short' and crumbly	Made up into layers. Very light and flaky.	Made up into layers. Forms a strong sheet that can be rolled. Very crisp, tougher than other forms of pastry.
Examples of use	Pie bases and tops	Pie crusts and sausage rolls	Samosas and strudels

Table 10 There are three main types of pastry. Each is suitable for enclosing different food substances.

pathogens are **bacteria** that can cause disease or food-poisoning if they are consumed in high enough numbers.

a **pre-mix** is a blend of minor ingredients for a recipe, such as spices, flavourings or **additives**, together with a small amount of one of the major ingredients. The pre-mix then becomes a major ingredient, making it much easier to ensure that each of the minor ingredients will be evenly distributed in the product.

preservatives are used to prevent food from spoiling due to the growth of **micro-organisms**. Permitted preservatives are given **E numbers** and the way in which they are used is strictly controlled.

Name of preservative	E number	Products the preservative is used in
Calcium propionate	E282	Bread
Potassium sorbate	E202	Reduced sugar jam, fruit pies
Sodium metabisulphite	E223	Fruit squash
Sodium benzoate	E211	Fizzy drinks

Table 11 Examples of preservatives and the foods they are used in

Sugar, salt and vinegar have also been used for many centuries to preserve food, but are not officially listed as preservatives and, therefore, do not have to be listed as such on a food **ingredients list**.

primary foods are obtained from directly harvested materials. Some primary foods go to the retail market after primary processing, but many will be sold on to other **manufacturers** as raw ingredients for secondary processing.

Examples of primary foods include wheat **flour**, milk, meat, fish, **maize**, **eggs**, fruit, vegetables, vegetable **oils** and **fats**.

Consider meat as an example of a primary food:

- When an animal is slaughtered its carcass is divided up. Some of the meat will be sold to the **consumer** as joints or as different cuts of meat. In this case the meat is a primary food.
- Some parts of the carcass will be sold on to another food manufacturer, to be used as an ingredient, for example, to make meat pies or sausages. The meat undergoes secondary processing and the meat pies and sausages are **secondary foods**.

product analysis provides useful information about the design and manufacture of existing food products. Product analysis includes the practical analysis of products and the collection of data from retail outlets.

Manufacturers undertake product analysis because it helps them to evaluate:

- the properties and uses of food ingredients
- the processes used to manufacture the product
- the **quality of design** and **quality of manufacture** achieved by other manufacturers
- the price ranges of products
- the suitability of the product for the **target market group**
- why the product is successful: compare with similar products that are available
- ideas for new products.

When you analyse a product you need to evaluate it using similar criteria that you use to develop a **design specification**:

- Explain the product's end-use, its function or purpose.
- State the target market group and describe their needs and values.
- Explain why the product is suitable for the target market group. Include references to any special features, such as the appeal of the **packaging design** and the value for money of the product.

> **In your coursework project you will need to:**
>
> - take account of the needs and values of a range of **consumers**
> - understand that changing food fashions, the price consumers will pay, **brand** image, lifestyle changes and **environmental issues** can influence the design and manufacture of food products.

- Describe what the product looks like – its **aesthetic** characteristics.
- Describe how well the product performs its stated role. Include reference to the nutritional value of the product.
- Is the product a new product? Has it been developed to respond to a particular market demand?
- List the ingredients used and explain their functions.
- What processes have been used in the manufacture of the product?

> **Coursework checkpoint: *product analysis***
>
> Analyse **batch** produced products (e.g. fizzy drinks; pizzas; canned soups) and **high volume** products (e.g. fish fingers; crisps) to find out why they are made by these different production methods.
>
> When you analyse a product remember to:
> - list the ingredients it contains in the order they are given
> - investigate the **nutritional information** given
> - work out how the product was made
> - decide on the target market group for the product.

In your coursework project you will need to understand:

- how systems are used in industry to control design and manufacture
- that systems are made up of inputs, processes and outputs.

Product Data Management (PDM) software is used to integrate the use of computer systems, including computer-aided design (CAD), computer-aided manufacture (CAM) and computer integrated manufacturing (CIM). The software organises and communicates accurate, up-to-date information in a database. Manufacturers and retailers can use Information and Communication Technology (ICT) and PDM software to monitor stock levels and sales data so that reordering and manufacture of fresh products occur as soon as they become necessary.

PDM software allows access to product information for each member of the **product development team**. When changes are made to the ingredients, **specification** or **costing**, the information can be automatically sent to each team member. This means that everyone, including the production department, sales, finance, raw materials purchasing department, and product development team is working with the latest information. PDM reduces the time taken to get new products to market and enables manufacturers to use **just in time (JIT) methods of production**.

PDM software allows communications, using ICT, between departments, manufacturers, suppliers and retailers anywhere in the world. Ingredients or equipment can be sourced from different countries. Alternatively, specifications can be sent instantly to another factory for a product to be made there, assuming they have the necessary raw materials, equipment and manufacturing skills available.

product development (PD) or designing for **manufacture** is very important in the food industry which is very competitive. **Manufacturers** are always trying to come up with new products to tempt people to buy their products. When one manufacturer comes up with something new, others have to develop a similar product or they will lose sales. Manufacturers also need to undertake **trend-forecasting** to spot fashions in eating and to respond rapidly to them.

Most product development is carried out to introduce new ingredients or new **flavours** into an existing range of foods. For example, a manufacturer may decide to develop a 'low-fat' alternative range of snack products to an existing range or to produce new flavours for potato crisps.

Generating ideas for trial products	Initial ideas can be generated from: • a design brief received from a customer (client, see page 89) • market research showing a gap in the market, such as for a new range of ethnic foods. Some manufacturers send a PD manager to investigate foods in another country, such as India or Mexico, to get ideas for new foods or ingredients. • a competitor's new product that needs to be matched • the manufacturer needing more products to keep the factory busy • product analysis carried out by the PD team. Team members produce a design specification and generate ideas for new products based on all the information they have collected.
Development of ideas	Basic recipes are developed and produced in the test kitchen. These are tested by the PD team and the best ones selected for more development work. A product prototype is developed.
Transfer to factory production	Production is transferred to large scale factory equipment (scaling-up). A product specification and a manufacturing process specification will be finalised, in collaboration with the production team. Packaging materials and design will be finalised and the order given to the packaging manufacturer for the packaging to be produced.
Product launch	Advertising may be used to promote the new product. The manufacturer waits to find out if the product will sell and if consumers will return for repeat purchases. Even with careful evaluation of ideas throughout the PD process, over 75% of new products fail to sell sufficiently to stay in production.

Table 12 There are a number of stages in the product development process

the **product development team** are the people who turn initial ideas into products that the company can produce and sell. The team members have specialist skills and may include:

- a development chef who is responsible for producing the product **prototype**. He or she may suggest different ingredients and preparation methods.
- a food **technologist** (see page 89) who is responsible for ensuring the prototype can be transferred to the factory for production
- a sales and **marketing** advisor who will make sure that the product is one that retailers will be willing to stock
- an ingredient purchasing specialist who knows where to source ingredients of the right **quality** at the best price
- a packaging technologist to advise on suitable **packaging materials** and **design**
- a sensory analyst who is responsible for making sure **consumers** in the **target market group** like the product
- a microbiologist, especially if the product is a **high risk** one
- a nutritionist, especially if the product is being promoted as 'healthy'.

a **product specification** is written for every product that the manufacturer produces. It gives all the information about the product. Information in the design specification will be used to help draw up the product specification. The product specification is held in the company's office. A manufacturing process specification is written using information in the product specification and this is used in the factory to direct production.

The product specification must contain details about:

- the product name, including a brief description of the product
- the name and address of the manufacturer
- a list of ingredients, including the names of suppliers
- storage conditions for ingredients
- standards to which the product must conform. This includes the target values, with tolerances, set for the quality indicators. Photographs may be included to define acceptable standards of colour, for example.
- nutritional information
- product selling weight
- packaging details
- storage information
- shelf life details.

In your coursework project you will need to:

- design a food product that could be manufactured in quantity
- choose the most suitable **method of production** for your food product and give reasons for choosing it
- understand what is meant by **high volume**, why it is used for manufacturing products and how it compares with other methods of production
- understand that **systems** are used in the food industry to control manufacture
- simulate a production line.

a **production line** is where food products are manufactured and packaged by teams of people, with each manufacturing process following one another in a line. In the food industry, food processing and packaging may be carried out in completely separate areas of the factory, depending on whether the product is high risk, or low risk. Many products need to be cooled, chilled or frozen before they are packaged, so packaging may be carried out several hours after the product is processed.

a **production line simulation** involves working as a production team to manufacture food products. Production simulation can also be achieved using computer software to develop and model products.

a **production plan** gives information about the type and quantity of products to be manufactured. Different production methods (custom made, batch, high volume) need different types of production plan. The production plan can be used to develop a schedule for manufacture.

The production plan includes:

- details of **raw materials** needed; the quantities they must be ordered in; their lead times. (The lead time is the length of time a material must be ordered before it is needed. The purchasing department will need this information.)
- the **manufacturing process specification** for the product
- details of all the manufacturing processes that will be needed, in the order they occur and the time that each is expected to take. The number of people needed for each operation should be included. This information will then provide the schedule for manufacture.
- details of any special arrangements for storage or transportation of the finished product, e.g. should transport be arranged for the day it is produced? (This may be the case for products such as sandwiches.)

Coursework checkpoint: *production plan*

1. Draw up a production plan for your next food product. Include the following information:
   ○ A manufacturing process specification with details of materials and components, and clear processing details.
   ○ A schedule for manufacture with details of manufacturing processes in their correct order. Include details of times and temperatures where these are needed.
   ○ A **flow chart** to show where and how you will check your product quality.
2. Use the information in your production plan to monitor the quality of your product, making checks at each stage of production.

In your coursework project you will need to:

- produce and use a production plan which details the manufacturing process specification and schedule for manufacture
- identify **critical control points (CCPs)** in the manufacturing process
- plan **quality** checks and **feedback** to help solve possible problems
- use a time plan to show how long each stage of manufacture will take.

production planning means working out the best order for producing different food products on a **production line**. Several different products may be made in one day. If there is only a slight difference between the products, e.g. different **flavours**, the production line can usually run continuously with a small amount of the product being discarded at the 'change-over'.

If the change is more major the production line will have to stop, for example, if there is a change in pack size or shape that needs different machinery to be fitted. This results in lost production time (known as 'downtime') and production staff try to minimise this through efficient planning.

Production planning must also take account of the order in which products are required for delivery. Many food products have a short **shelf life**, so they are often made and loaded immediately on to lorries for distribution. Products needed for early loading may have to be made first, even if this increases the downtime.

a **production system** (method of production, manufacturing system, method of manufacture, scale of production) is decided by the type and amount of product to be made. Production systems enable **manufacturers** to produce food products quickly and efficiently and can include:

- one-off production
- batch production
- high volume (mass production)
- continuous production.

protein is an essential nutrient in the human diet. It is needed for the building and repair of cells, so is very important for a growing child. The other main use of protein is in the formation of **enzymes**, which play a part in the chemical reactions that govern everything that happens within the body. Any surplus protein from the diet is used by the body for energy.

Proteins have a number of **functional properties** in foods:

- They coagulate or 'set' when they are heated. An **egg** white sets when you fry or boil it. This makes the protein easier to digest.
- Proteins (gluten) in wheat **flour** trap gas and allow bread to rise. When the bread is baked, the proteins set and give shape and volume to the bread.

- Proteins in egg white coagulate when they are whipped, trapping air and forming a foam for a meringue or a mousse.
- Proteins (enzymes) from some fruits, such as papain that comes from the papaya plant, can be used to tenderise meat.
- Proteins can react with some **sugars** to make some foods brown. Chips and crisps would be pale and unattractive without this reaction, which involves the protein and sugar naturally present in potatoes.
- Proteins will coagulate if their pH is changed to a particular value. This method is used to make milk proteins coagulate when yoghurt is made.

a **prototype** is an initial product developed during product development (PD), once the initial design specification has been drawn up. The prototype may be modified to take account of feedback from sensory evaluation or to make it match the design specification more closely.

> **In your coursework project you will need to:**
> - develop a prototype for your food product
> - use **sensory analysis** to gain feedback about the sensory characteristics of your product
> - use test methods to gain information about your product
> - respond to the information you have gained, to modify your product as necessary.

quality means meeting set standards, to make consistent food products that always meet the product specification. When developing a quality product a manufacturer must produce the right product for the right customer at the right price. The product development team needs to consider fitness for purpose, value for money, the selection of raw ingredients and the method of production.

1. Quality for the consumer means a product's fitness-for-purpose. This can be evaluated through price, aesthetic appeal and ability to meet the consumer's nutritional needs.
2. Quality for a manufacturer means meeting the product specification and finding a balance between the following:
   - Profitable manufacture of consistent products on time and to budget.
   - The needs and expectations of the consumer and environment.
3. High quality design and manufacturing result in a higher level of quality and products that sell at a higher price. This requires high levels of training and skills and the prevention of faults through the use of quality assurance (QA) systems.
4. Low quality design and manufacturing result in poor quality products that can only be sold at low prices. Low quality manufacturing results in high levels of waste or rework.

> **In your coursework project you will need to:**
> - understand that the quality of a product can be judged by the appropriate use of ingredients and equipment, how easy the product is to manufacture, its fitness for purpose and its impact on the environment
> - evaluate the quality of your food product against the product specification, to make sure that it is suitable for your intended consumer(s)
> - modify your product where appropriate to improve its quality so it meets the needs of your **target market group**.

quality assurance (QA) is used in a quality system that is planned to make sure that food products match the product specification. The aim of QA is to make a consistent product with no rejects. This enables manufacturers to sell high quality food products at a profit to consumers.

QA systems are planned to monitor every stage of design and manufacture. QA uses standards, testing procedures and processes that are appropriate to the product being made. QA makes use of written procedures and systems to prevent faults before they can arise. QA measures include the use of:

> **In your coursework project you will need to:**
> - understand the difference between QC and QA
> - understand how a QA system is used in manufacturing food in quantity.

- inspection of suppliers' premises and work practices to ensure that the ingredients they supply will be satisfactory
- detailed specifications
- **costing** sheets
- work schedules
- **computer systems**
- **quality control (QC)** systems
- standard working processes and practices
- inspection and fault finding.

A QA system requires a team of people working together and sharing information about the product. This often results in vast amounts of documentation and paperwork. Many manufacturers use **Product Data Management (PDM)** software to monitor quality and production. PDM also enables the whole management and production teams to have up-to-date information about the product.

quality control (QC) is used to test and monitor the manufacture of food products. QC involves checking the product at identified points, including **critical control points (CCPs)** for conformance to permitted **tolerance** ranges that are in the **specification**. This ensures that the product meets **consumer** expectations. QC test methods, checks and inspection processes enable the manufacture of consistent products with no rejects.

QC is the practical way of achieving **quality assurance (QA)**. QC is the responsibility of everyone in the production team and it:

- makes use of specifications and standards to monitor **quality**
- makes use of inspection to identify faults
- is applied to **raw materials** (ingredients and **packaging materials**), design, production and the finished product
- provides **feedback** to the QA system, to make sure that it is working properly.

1. Incoming raw materials (ingredients and packaging materials) are checked, tested and stored as set out in the QA system.
2. The **product development (PD)** and production departments develop specifications and documents that provide information such as:

- product recipe
- **method of production**
- **flow chart** showing manufacturing processes and conditions (for example, the times and temperatures needed) and CCPs
- QC tests and procedures
- **quality indicators**
- steps to be taken if a quality indicator test result is outside its allowed tolerance
- packaging to be used
- permitted nett weight and tolerances
- storage conditions.

Coursework checkpoint: *quality control (QC)*
Remember to record any changes you need to make to the design, manufacturing processes or packaging of your product. This will enable you to explain how you could manufacture consistent products in **high volume**.

In your coursework project you will need to:

- understand the difference between QC and QA
- use your **product specification** to evaluate the quality of your product
- use QC to check your product for faults
- specify in your **production plan** how you will check for quality
- use QC and feedback to help solve possible problems in your product manufacture.

In your coursework project you will need to:
■ use QC techniques during the manufacture of your food product
■ use quality indicators to check the quality of your product at specified points during its manufacture
■ evaluate your product to make sure it is suitable for your target **consumers**.

quality indicators are used at specified points during production to check that the quality of the product is conforming to the **product specification**. These points may be **critical control points (CCPs)**, but quality checks may also be carried out in places that are not CCPs. Quality indicators are either variables or attributes.

- Variables are direct measurements such as the weight of a product or the temperature of food in a cooking pan.
- Attributes are either right or wrong, such as the **colour** of a biscuit or the way topping is distributed on top of a pizza.

In a food **quality control (QC)** system, quality indicators must have target values that the **manufacturer** is trying to achieve for both variables and attributes. There must also be **tolerances**, as it is not possible in food manufacture always to achieve a target value, due to the variable nature of food materials.

quality of design measures how well a newly developed food product matches up to the original **design brief**. Good quality of design means that a product will sell successfully. If the product design is poor then the product will not sell, even if it is well manufactured. For example, fresh cream cakes with a luxury filling designed to sell to affluent single people and couples will not sell if they are only available in 'family size' packs. Good quality of design refers to a food product that:

- is well designed and attractive to the **target market group**
- matches the design brief
- uses suitable ingredients
- is easy to manufacture
- can be marketed at a price the **consumer** is willing to pay.

In your coursework project you will need to:
■ understand the difference between quality of design and **quality of manufacture**
■ understand that the **quality** of a product can be judged by how far it meets consumer needs, the appropriate use of materials and components, its **fitness for purpose** and its impact on the environment.

quality of manufacture measures how well a product matches its product specification. If quality of manufacture is poor then the product will have faults and may have to be scrapped. If it is sent to the shops, **consumers** may not like it. For example, if the wrong amount of stabiliser is added to a fruit drink it might be thick and unpleasant to drink. Consumers would not wish to buy the product again.

Good quality of manufacture refers to a food product that:

- is well made, using suitable ingredients
- matches the **product specification**
- is manufactured using a suitable, safe production method
- is made within budget limits to sell at an attractive price to the target market group.

In your coursework project you will need to:
■ understand the difference between **quality of design** and quality of manufacture
■ understand that the **quality** of a product can be judged by how far it meets user needs.

a **quality system** is used by food **manufacturers** to control the quality of all the company's activities. Quality assurance (QA) and quality control (QC) are both components of the company's quality system.

raising agents are used in baking to increase the volume of products. This makes them less dense and therefore 'lighter' and more pleasant to eat. Carbon dioxide (CO_2) is used to make the products rise. There are two methods used to generate the CO_2.

1. Chemical raising agents can be purchased as baking powder and used in products such as cakes and scones. Alternatively, self-raising **flour** can be used. This contains chemical raising agents added to the flour in the correct proportions. Sodium hydrogen carbonate (also known as sodium bicarbonate) and an acid such as acid calcium phosphate (ACP) or tartaric acid react to produce CO_2. The reaction occurs mostly when the product is heated, so that cakes rise when they are baked.

2. Yeast is a naturally occurring **micro-organism**. It is used as the raising agent in bread and products such as hot cross buns. **Enzymes** in the yeast ferment **sugars** to produce CO_2. The yeast is killed during baking and so time is needed to produce the CO_2 before the dough enters the oven. In bread making this happens when the dough is proved. Yeast-leavened (raised) products use flour with more **protein** (gluten) than chemically-raised goods and this gives them a tougher **texture**.

Coursework checkpoint: *raising agents*

- Yeast is used to make bread rise. Try making bread using self-raising flour and no yeast. Check the difference in volume, texture and **taste** compared to a loaf made with yeast.
- Baking powder and self-raising flour are used to make scones rise. Try using plain flour and yeast in a scone recipe. Compare the result with scones made with self-raising flour and baking powder.

raw materials are the ingredients and components that a food factory needs to convert into its final products. Incoming lorries are directed to a special 'intake' area where the raw materials are inspected, off-loaded and placed immediately into stores at the correct temperature. **Sampling** and **testing** are often carried out before the ingredients are accepted for delivery.

Availability and cost of raw ingredients is important when deciding on ideas for new products.

- Most fruits, vegetables and cereals are harvested only once a year, so companies may need to source ingredients from different countries in order to have a continuous supply. This means that **texture**, **taste** and **flavour** of the ingredients may vary through the year, making it very difficult to produce a consistent **quality** product.

    To avoid this problem, some **manufacturers** (see page 89) may always use a preserved ingredient instead of a fresh one. For example, canned apple pieces might be used in apple pies, rather than fresh apples, to make sure the product is always the same.

- Alternatively, some manufacturers, for example, of fresh soups, use *only* fresh ingredients. They make each variety of soup for a very limited period each year.

In your coursework project you will need to understand:

- the properties and characteristics of food raw materials
- that food ingredients can be cut, shaped, combined and processed to create more useful properties
- that the properties of the finished product should be suitable for the intended **consumers** (see page 89).

> **Coursework checkpoint:** *raw materials*
>
> Food raw materials can be used in different ways to change the characteristics of the products you design. Try experimenting with different **size reduction** methods to change the **appearance** and **aesthetic** appeal of a fruit salad, or a vegetable salad. Use **finishing processes** to add a garnish and add aesthetic value to a product.

Recommended Daily Amount (RDA) is the amount of energy and nutrients suitable for different groups of people. It is sometimes written as Recommended Daily Allowance. RDA values are the same as the Recommended Nutrient Intake (RNI) values.

Recommended Nutrient Intake (RNI) values are set by the Department of Health for different age/sex groups. They give the amount of **protein**, **vitamins** and **minerals** that are enough, or more than enough, for 97% of the people in that group.

	Protein g/day	Thiamin mg/day	Riboflavin mg/day	Vitamin C mg/day	Calcium mg/day	Iron mg/day
Girls aged 11–14	41.2	0.7	1.2	35	800	14.8
Girls aged 15–18	45.0	0.8	1.1	40	800	14.8
Boys aged 11–14	42.1	0.9	1.2	35	1000	11.3
Boys aged 15–18	55.2	1.1	1.3	40	1000	11.3

Table 13 RNI values for protein, vitamins and iron for 11–18 year olds

risk assessment is a formal practice used in all industrial situations. Every process must be considered, to establish:

- what could go wrong to create a **hazard** for operators, for the product or for the environment
- what are the chances of this particular hazard occurring.

Suitable procedures must be put in place to ensure that the risk is either eliminated or, if that is not possible, that it is reduced to a minimum. Written procedures should also be in place to deal with the hazard if it does arise.

Risk assessment should also be used in a kitchen, since sharp knives, hot liquids, ovens, and food spillages can all present hazards.

Design brief	Initial risk assessment: check safety standards, regulations and legislation
Design specification	Include safety criteria and quality control (QC) procedures
Design ideas	Risk assessment for each idea: check against the design specification
Product specification	Storage conditions for ingredients, product storage information and shelf life details
Manufacturing process specification	Include safety criteria and critical control points (CCPs)
Prototype	Risk assessment: test prototype against safety criteria in the manufacturing process and against food safety legislation. Check safety of product in conditions where customers do not store it or use it exactly as directed (known as consumer abuse).
Manufacturing process	Risk assessment of materials, processes and equipment: use of QC procedures
Final product	Risk assessment: test final product against legislation. Check for safety under conditions of consumer abuse.

Table 14 Risk assessment is carried out at the key stages in the design and manufacture of a product

Coursework checkpoint: *risk assessment*

You need to think about risk assessment when designing and making your food product.

1. Draw up a chart to show the key stages in the design and manufacture of your food product.
2. For each stage, list the potential hazards and assess the risks associated with them.
3. Write safety procedures to eliminate or reduce the risk for each potential hazard.

In your coursework project you will need to:

- include safety criteria in your **specifications**
- take responsibility for recognising hazards in manufacturing processes and work areas
- care for yourself and others in a manufacturing environment
- use safety information to help you assess risks involved in designing, making and using food products
- follow safety rules to reduce risks when designing and making food products
- check the safety of your product so it is safe for your intended **consumer**
- explain how to manage your working environment so you keep risks under control.

sampling is used in quality control (QC) testing as it is not possible to test every food item to make sure that it is satisfactory. A sample that is taken and used for analysis *must* be truly representative. If it is not, then the results of any tests carried out on it will not reflect the quality of the whole.

Samples taken from a production line should be taken at regular intervals from a continuous production run. For a batch run they should be taken from (for example) the beginning, the middle and the end. The bigger the batch, the more samples need to be taken.

scaling-up is used to transfer the manufacture of a product from the kitchen or pilot plant to the factory. It is a stage in the product development (PD) process.

Kitchen-scale	Factory-scale	Comments
Ingredients:		
500g fresh, washed fruit 500g sugar	100kg cleaned fruit 140kg glucose syrup 140kg sugar 30kg pectin solution 3kg acidity regulator solution 50kg water Artificial colour (optional)	Factory might use fresh fruit, but probably frozen or puréed fruit. This would allow jam making all year round – not just when the fruit is in season. Pectin and acidity regulator ensure consistent product quality.
Processing:		
Cook fruit gently in a pan on cooking hob. Add sugar, mix in and heat to a rolling boil.	Add all ingredients to a steam-heated tank fitted with an automatic stirrer, and heat	Stirrer prevents mixture from sticking to the tank
Testing:		
Check concentration of sugar and fruit solids is right for jam to form a gel by removing a little jam, cooling it and seeing if it is setting	After a set cooking time, check pH of jam and measure solids using a refractometer	Use of objective testing ensures consistent quality product
Packaging:		
When jam is ready, pour into hot jars and cover immediately	Pump product from tank to a filler tank, and deposit automatically into jars. Seal jars immediately after filling.	Use of standard pectin solution ensures fruit will not all rise to top of jar

Table 15 How jam production would alter from kitchen-scale to factory-scale

When scaling-up a product the development team will need to consider:

- the weights of ingredients needed for large-scale production. These will need to be ordered and stored in sufficient quantities.
- the number of staff needed to manage all the processes
- the type and frequency of **quality control (QC)** tests that will need to be carried out during production
- the large-scale equipment that will be needed and how its use will affect the process, compared to kitchen-scale production. For example, **mixing** times will need to be altered to take account of the larger amount of ingredients. Some companies find that using factory machinery instead of kitchen equipment can change the characteristics of their products. To avoid this problem they do all the product development work in the factory itself rather than in a test kitchen.

the **schedule for manufacture** forms part of the production plan. It is used by the production planning team to help them calculate the materials, equipment and time that will be needed to make the required amount of the product when it is ordered by a customer.

The schedule for manufacture includes details about:

- the product recipe
- preparation of ingredients (for example, cutting vegetables to size, or weighing and mixing spices and other **additives**)
- all processes (including machine settings, and time and temperature settings as appropriate)
- manpower needed to make the product
- estimated time needed to complete each task.

> **Coursework checkpoint:** *schedule for manufacture*
>
> Remember that a schedule for manufacture is *part* of your production plan.
>
> Remember to record any changes you make when making your product. This will enable you to explain how you could manufacture identical products in **high volume**.

secondary foods are products where a number of raw ingredients have been combined to make a food product. Examples include meat pies, breakfast cereals, bread and ready-meals. The type of ingredients used and the way in which they are processed will decide the characteristics of the end product.

sensory analysis involves using people to test food. Manufacturers (see page 89) use scientific instruments to analyse food wherever possible as these provide objective data and the analysis can easily be repeated. Scientific instruments are available at any time of the day or night and they don't have 'off' days.

However, it is *people* who buy and eat food so manufacturers also need to know what they think about their food. A group of people, known as a '**sensory panel**' or '**taste** panel', is brought together to test the food. Sensory analysis can include using all five senses, including taste, sight, touch, smell and sound to test food.

In your coursework project you will need to:

- produce and use a detailed schedule for manufacture for making your product.

Food samples presented to a taste panel should always be identified by random numbers or letters, so as not to suggest to the panellists that there is any order to them. This might influence their decisions. Any packaging that shows the manufacturer's name should be hidden from view, again to avoid any bias. Sensory analysis should be carried out in an area where the panellists can be quiet, in order for them to concentrate and make up their own minds about the food, rather than talking to other panellists.

Sensory analysis can be used in a number of ways.

1 To rank food products in order of some characteristic, such as 'consumer liking'. Table 16 shows a form that could be given to members of a sensory panel to find out which recipe for a jacket potato filling they like most. Scores from all the panellists are added up. The sample with the highest score is the most popular.

Please taste the three samples of jacket potato filling you have been given.
Please cleanse your mouth using water between tasting each sample.
For each sample, please give a score between 1 and 5, using the following scale:
1 = dislike a lot
2 = dislike a bit
3 = neither like nor dislike
4 = like a little
5 = like a lot

	Sample JBX	Sample KWI	Sample MZV
Score			

Table 16 Sensory panel form

2 To identify the important characteristics of foods, such as to describe their taste or **flavour**. Panellists can be given a list of flavour description words and asked which one(s) fit the food samples. For example, panel members tasting two similar strawberry-flavoured desserts could be given the following list of words:
   - Savoury
   - Fruity
   - Sweet
   - Acidic
   - Tasteless
   - Weak
   - Strong
   - Spicy

   They would then be asked to tick the words that describe how each food tastes to them.

3 To identify the difference between two food products. This test can be used when a manufacturer is trying to produce a new food product that matches that of a competitor.
   - Panellists are given three food samples, two of which are the competitor's product and the third one is the new product.
   - The panellists are asked to spot the 'odd' food sample. All the food samples must look the same or there is no point asking anyone to taste them to find the difference!
   - The more people who correctly identify the 'odd' sample, the greater the difference between the competitor's product and the new product.

> **In your coursework project you will need to:**
>
> - identify how you could use sensory analysis to get **feedback** on your product from your **target market group**
> - use **Information and Communication Technology (ICT)** to produce questionnaires to find out information from a sensory panel
> - be prepared to adapt your product in response to sensory analysis feedback.

a sensory panel (taste panel) is a group of people who use their five senses to undertake the sensory analysis of food. Sensory panels can be trained or untrained.

- Untrained sensory panels are asked to taste food as **consumers** (see page 89). They can say if they like or dislike a particular aspect of the food, such as flavour, or which food they like best. They can also be asked to describe food in general terms or to identify the difference between two food samples.
- Trained sensory panels are used by some food **manufacturers** to provide in-depth analysis of the sensory attributes of foods.

the **setting** of foods can be achieved in two ways:

1. Using processing conditions that make **proteins** in the food set. This is used in products such as:
   - bread, where the use of heat during baking makes the **flour** proteins set
   - cake, where the use of heat during baking makes the **egg** proteins set.

   These two products are known to food **technologists** as solid foams.

2. Creating a **gel** in the food. This is used in products such as:
   - blancmange, where **starch** is the gelling agent
   - jams, where pectin is the gelling agent
   - some pies and confectionery, where gelatin is the gelling agent.

shelf life is the length of time that food will last without deteriorating in quality. Deterioration in quality might mean:

- a risk that the food has become unsafe to eat
- a risk that the food is beginning to spoil or go 'off'
- a loss of palatability – the food loses its attractive **taste** or **texture**
- some loss of nutrients, due to reactions occurring within the food.

By law, foods must be marked with either a 'best before' or a 'use by' date. 'Best before' is used for foods which will eventually lose palatability or nutritional value, such as canned foods, frozen foods and bread (which will go stale).

'Use by' is used for foods that have only a short shelf life. These are mainly chilled foods, such as cut salads, cream cakes or pizzas. 'Use by' is used for **high risk** foods, that become unsafe to eat if they are kept too long. Sometimes they have a 'sell by' or 'display until' date on the label as well. This is not required by law, but is used for the convenience of the supermarket to help them remove old stock.

Food labels showing 'best before' and 'use by' date marking systems

shortening is the fat or blend of fats used for making shortcrust pastry and biscuits. The shortening coats the flour particles and stops flour proteins (gluten) from joining together, which would result in a tough 'bite' to the product. A manufacturer chooses a shortening that is soft enough (sufficiently 'plastic') at the right temperature for this process. Shortening also affects the texture, flavour, mouthfeel and colour of the product.

> **Coursework checkpoint:** *shortening*
> 1. Use different shortenings (e.g. margarine, butter, vegetarian lard) to make cakes or scones.
> 2. Investigate the difference each type of shortening makes to your product (**taste**, flavour or texture).

size reduction describes a unit operation that is used to reduce the size of food materials. Size reduction operations include:
- chopping
- crushing
- cutting
- grinding
- mashing
- milling
- mincing
- slicing
- shredding.

Size reduction is used for many types of food ingredients. For example:
- whole carrots are cleaned and peeled, then sliced or diced for use in soups
- whole apples are peeled, then sliced or diced for use in pies and tarts
- milling is needed to produce flour from wheat
- meat must be minced before it is used in sausages and burgers, so that it will mix properly with other ingredients
- potatoes must be sliced thinly to make crisps (see flow chart on page 76)
- in canned foods, the food pieces must be small enough to go into the cans. If the food pieces are too large the heating (**sterilisation**) process will take longer and there will be more change in the texture of the food.
- products such as joints of meat or fish fillets are cut to the size required for sale.

The equipment used for size reduction depends on the food type. In general, moist foods such as vegetables and meat can be chopped, cut, sliced and shredded. Dry foods like wheat or spices must be ground, crushed or milled. Fruits are also crushed when they are having juice extracted from them.

> **In your coursework project you will need to:**
> - select suitable tools, equipment and processes to make products that match a **specification**
> - use tools and equipment efficiently to achieve a well-made product
> - work safely with materials and equipment when designing and making your product.

How potato crisps are made

Intake
Potatoes are received from a merchant already cleaned and washed and ready to be used

↓

Peeling
A thin layer of peel is removed from the potatoes by machine. The less peel is removed the higher the yield of crisps from the potatoes.

↓

Slicing
Potatoes are sliced by machine. This is a size reduction operation.

↓

Washing
The potato slices are sprayed with water to remove loose starch. The slices move on to a moving conveyor belt.

↓

Drying
The conveyor takes the slices past jets of air that dry them. The air jets are known as 'air knives'.

↓

Frying
The potato slices pass through a continuous fryer – a long shallow bath containing hot oil. The crisps leave the fryer on a mesh conveyor so that excess oil can drop off.

↓

Cooling
The crisps cool as they travel on the conveyor to the seasoning stage

↓

Seasoning
The seasoning mix is metered continuously into a seasoning drum. The drum rotates and the crisps move around as they pass through. The seasoning sticks to the crisps as the oil on them is still slightly warm.

↓

Weighing
The crisps pass into an automatic weighing machine. Small amounts of crisps fall into pockets in the machine. The computer selects pockets that can join together to give the required weight of crisps.

↓

Packaging
The crisps are dropped into a bag as it is being formed on the packaging machine. Air is removed from the bag and replaced by nitrogen. This helps to extend the shelf life of the crisps.

↓

Checkweighing
Ensures the correct nett weight in the packet. (This is the weight of crisps that is shown on the packet.)

↓

Metal detecting
Ensures the packets contain no metal fragments

↓

Date coding
Crisp packets are marked with a 'best before' date and a code giving manufacturing details

↓

Packaging into boxes
A number of packets are filled into cardboard boxes to make distribution easier. The cardboard boxes are the secondary packaging for the crisps.

↓

Storage
At ambient temperature

↓

Distribution
At ambient temperature

How potato crisps are made including a size reduction stage

A **smart food** is a term used in education to describe food materials that have been developed to fulfil a specific functional role. Examples include modified starches, low-fat spreads and artificial sweeteners. The term 'smart food' is not widely used within the food industry.

specifications are used to specify the design and manufacturing criteria of food products and are used to monitor quality.

A **design specification** guides a designer's thinking about what is to be designed. It is used to guide research, to test and evaluate design ideas and to develop the manufacturing process specification.

A manufacturing process specification ensures that a food product is manufactured as the designer intends. It forms part of the production plan for the manufacture of a food product. The manufacturing process specification is used on the factory floor to direct production and as a standard for checking the quality of each product. The information in the manufacturing process specification is written using information in the product specification. The product specification holds *all* the information about the product. It is held in the office and is a confidential document within the company.

> **In your coursework project you will need to:**
>
> - develop and use detailed design specification criteria
> - use your design specification to generate, test and evaluate design ideas
> - use your manufacturing process specification to evaluate the quality of your product.

Design specification	Manufacturing process specification
Developed from the design brief, research and analysis	Developed from the design specification and the product specification
Specifies the design development	Specifies the product manufacture
Used to generate, test and evaluate design ideas	Used to test and evaluate product manufacture
Used to monitor the quality of design	Used to monitor the quality of manufacture
Used to develop a product specification and a manufacturing process specification	Used to develop a quality product

Table 17 The differences between a design specification and a manufacturing process specification

stabilisers are additives and are given E numbers. Stabilisers are used together with emulsifiers to maintain an emulsion once it has been formed. They are also used to thicken products, as their molecules bind large quantities of water.

Name of stabiliser	E number	Uses
Pectin	E440	Added to some fruit drinks to give 'body' to the drink
Xanthan gum	E415	Used to stabilise and thicken the emulsion in salad cream and some sauces
Guar gum Sodium alginate Carrageenan	E412 E401 E407	These are used to bind the water in ice-cream, so that no large ice crystals are formed when the ice-cream is frozen. This gives it a much smoother texture.

Table 18 Some examples of stabilisers and the products they can be used in

Understanding Industrial Practices: Food Technology © Nelson Thornes 2005

> **In your coursework project you will need to:**
>
> ■ produce and use a **schedule for manufacture** which shows the stages of production for your food product.

the **stages of production** for most food products include preparation, processing, **assembly**, **finishing**, packaging and storage.

Preparation can include, for example:

- the buying-in and **testing** of ingredients and components
- the preparation of ingredients for processing, e.g. weighing out, cleaning, peeling, preliminary **size-reduction**, pre-mixing of minor ingredients
- setting up machinery for the product to be made.

Processing can include, for example:

- **mixing** major ingredients
- **heat processing**, **chilling**, **freezing** or drying.

Assembly can include, for example:

- bringing different parts of a product together, by machine or by hand, e.g., adding meat or vegetable pieces to a pizza topping.

Finishing can include, for example:

- adding a garnish such as chopped herbs to improve the **aesthetic quality** of the product
- adding icing to the top of a cake. This will affect its **appearance**, **taste** and value.

Packaging can include, for example:

- placing the food product into its primary packaging
- adding a date code and a **label** to the primary packaging (if details of the product are not given on the packaging itself)
- collecting the packages into groups and placing them into secondary packaging
- date coding the secondary packaging.

Storage can include, for example:

- keeping the packaged product in a suitable storage area
- ensuring good stock rotation so that the oldest product is always sent out first to retail outlets.

> **In your coursework project you will need to:**
>
> ■ use standard components to make your manufacture easier and more cost-effective.

standard components are bought-in from other **manufacturers** to simplify production and help produce uniform food products. Standard food components can include, for example, a flavours **pre-mix** for a snack product, ready-chopped onions and diced meat for pies or canned fruit pieces for use in fruit yoghurt.

Suppliers of standard food components specialise in their production. This means the food product manufacturer:

- can be sure of buying a standard component of the right **quality** every time
- doesn't need to buy machinery that may be used when only one type of product is made
- doesn't have the problem of disposing of waste from the processing of raw ingredients
- can order standard components **just in time (JIT)** for production.

starch, a carbohydrate, is an important food ingredient with useful functional properties, such as its ability to form a gel in foods. Starch gels are widely used in the food industry and form the basis of blancmanges, custard, gravy and instant desserts. Most starch is extracted from maize and is known as cornflour.

Starch from maize, or other sources such as potatoes or tapioca, can be treated to form modified starches, which provide food manufacturers with a wide range of different starch products. Manufacturers can select a modified starch that will work in the way they want under the conditions that are right for the product. For example:

- using modified starch in the gravy of a pie that is to be frozen will make sure that the gravy is not thin and watery when the consumer eats the pie.

the **sterilisation** of food is carried out using heat treatment to destroy the micro-organisms present in the food. Sterilisation is carried out at temperatures in excess of 100°C so steam is the heating medium normally used. Although sterilisation brings about more changes to the sensory and nutritional quality of food than pasteurisation, it gives the food a much longer shelf life. Sterilised food can be stored at ambient temperature. Canning and Ultra High Temperature (UHT) processing are both examples of sterilisation.

the crystalline **sugar** used in the home is called sucrose. Sucrose, glucose, fructose and invert sugar are used in food manufacture. Dextrose is a form of glucose. In the food industry, dextrose and glucose are often used as syrups. There is then no need to dissolve the sugar crystals when a food product is made.

Sugar has a number of functions in food manufacture:

1 To provide sweetness.
   Foods such as baked beans, fruit pies and some sauces contain sugar to make them more attractive to the consumer. Artificial sweeteners can be used to provide sweetness and replace sugar in foods. Many manufacturers now make 'low sugar' or 'no added sugar' products, in response to consumer concerns about sugar intake.

2 To add colour.
   Some sugars that are naturally present in foods react with protein molecules when they are heated. This reaction is responsible for the attractive brown colouring of cooked meat and chips and many more products. Manufacturers can also influence the colour of products such as biscuits by choosing which sugar to use in their recipe. Sugar can also caramelise when it is heated strongly. Caramel is a sweet, sticky brown substance that is used to colour and flavour dessert products.

3 In preservation.
   Sugar bonds with water molecules present in food. The water is then not available for micro-organisms to use, so they cannot grow and the food does not spoil. This principle is used to preserve jam.

4 To add texture.
   Sugar crystals are used to give a slightly crunchy texture and gritty mouthfeel to confectionery such as fudge and fruit pastilles. Sugar also affects the hardness of biscuits. For example, ginger biscuits are very hard as they contain a high level of sugar.

In your coursework project you will need to:

- understand how systems are used in industry to control design and manufacture
- understand that systems are made up of inputs, processes and outputs and that feedback is used to make a system work well
- use a **quality control (QC)** system that incorporates feedback so your product is fault-free
- incorporate feedback into your own system
- use feedback from your user(s) to help you improve your product.

a **system** is a co-ordinated arrangement of activities working together in which inputs are processed to achieve outputs.

In a simple food manufacturing system for example, the INPUTS are food ingredients, **packaging materials**, labour, energy, time and machinery. The PROCESS is manufacturing the product and the OUTPUT is finished food products delivered to the customer and any waste or by-products that may be formed during the process. This way of thinking about manufacturing activities is called 'systems thinking'. A simple manufacturing system can be represented by a systems diagram (block diagram, **flow chart**) which shows how the system works. In this kind of simple system there is no **feedback** of information so it is called an 'open loop' system.

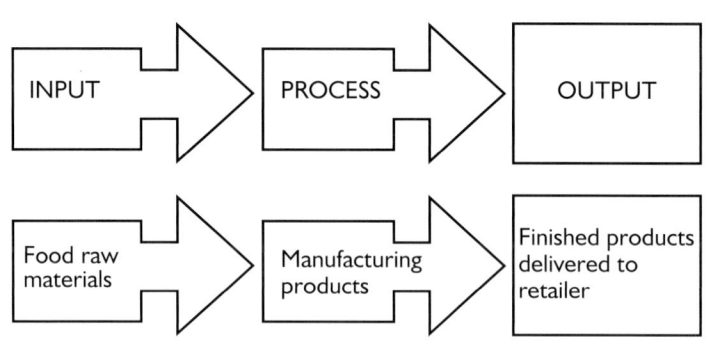

Block diagram to show a simple 'open loop' manufacturing system

A system that works well incorporates the feedback of information. This is called a 'closed loop' system. For example, **Information and Communication Technology** (ICT) systems allow the feedback of product sales information from **Electronic Point of Sale (EPOS)** tills to the food **manufacturer**. This feedback of information helps the manufacturer to plan production and manufacture goods to order.

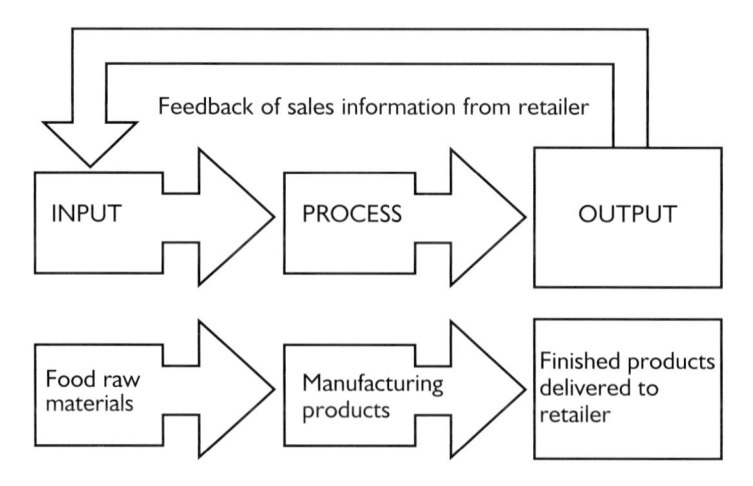

Block diagram to show a 'closed loop' manufacturing system

Large manufacturing systems are often made up of smaller sub-systems, such as product design, purchase of **raw materials**, production, stock control, sales and **marketing**. These can be linked together to make the whole system work in a cost-effective way. This linking is possible through the use of **Product Data Management (PDM)** software to enable **computer integrated manufacturing (CIM)**.

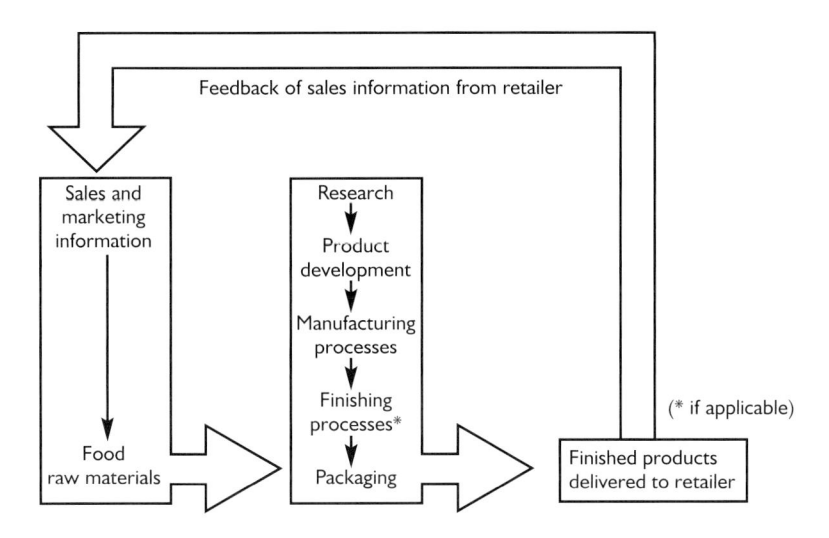

Block diagram to show a large manufacturing system with sub-systems

Types of systems used in food manufacturing include:
- **computer systems**
- **control systems**
- **costing** systems
- delivery systems
- ICT systems
- manufacturing systems
- marketing systems
- PDM systems
- production systems
- **quality systems**
- safety systems.

systems and control is a term used to explain how **systems, control systems, computer systems, quality systems** and **production systems** are used in food manufacturing. Different types of systems and control are used to monitor the whole manufacturing process so that products are manufactured efficiently at a profit.

the **target market group** is the consumer group that a manufacturer aims to sell to. Manufacturers use market research to identify the requirements and size of the target market group so that their food products will reflect the needs of the consumer. Target market groups can be identified according to age, quality needs, leisure activities and lifestyle.

Typical target market groups might include:
- children, who influence buying behaviour through 'pester power'
- teenagers and young adults
- young single workers and couples with no children
- young families with working mothers
- older family groups
- elderly single people or couples
- people with special nutritional needs.

In your coursework project you will need to:

- take account of the needs of a range of consumers.

the **taste** of food is detected by the taste buds on the tongue and at the back of the roof of the mouth. The taste of food is usually a blend of two or more of the following basic taste sensations:

- Sweetness (sugary substances).
- Sourness (acids, e.g. in citrus fruits or yoghurt).
- Bitterness (e.g. black coffee).
- Salt (e.g. salted crisps).

Food temperature affects taste. It is much more difficult to taste cold foods, so ice-cream must have more flavouring added to it than non-frozen desserts.

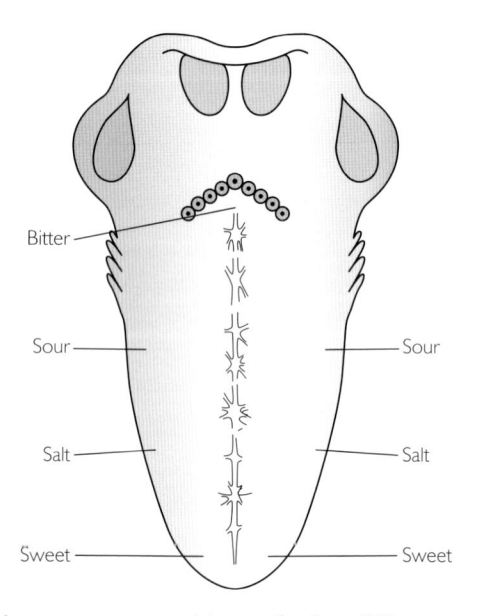

Different areas of the tongue are sensitive to the four different tastes

In your coursework project you will need to:

- choose the most suitable **method of production** for your product and give reasons for choosing it
- understand why teamwork improves product quality and output
- simulate a production line.

teamwork in manufacturing is a way of achieving more flexibility of production, a faster time to market and improved working conditions for employees. It has been defined by the Centre for Work and Technology as: 'a flexible, quick response system, consisting of self-organised, self-motivated, multi-skilled, versatile personnel who work collectively in teams, making joint decisions and sharing responsibility for output in terms of both **quality** and quantity.'

In the food industry teamwork can take different forms:

- In a **production line** or department arrangement each team member may learn every operation that is needed on that line, so that workers can sometimes move around, rather than do the same job all the time.
- In a factory-wide arrangement, teams may have members from different departments. They will work together to make suggestions to improve the overall running of the factory.

1 Benefits of teamwork to the **manufacturer**:
   - a flexible, multi-skilled workforce
   - increased productivity and efficiency
   - retained orders from retailers, through reliability
   - improved quality, through team responsibility
   - reduced absenteeism, through greater commitment to work
   - reduced labour turnover, through improved working conditions, giving an experienced, competent workforce.

2 Benefits of teamwork to the workforce:
- improved working conditions
- opportunities for decision making, to solve problems
- greater variety so less boredom
- increased average earnings
- improved relations with management
- increased motivation because workforce is multi-skilled.

3 Benefits of teamwork to consumers:
- improved product quality, through team responsibility
- improved delivery performance due to speed of manufacture
- fast response to customer demand, through flexibility.

48

testing of raw materials, equipment and products while they are being manufactured is an essential part of a quality assurance (QA) system. Tests must be carried out in a standard way and under controlled conditions, following a written test method. This ensures that the results obtained are reliable and the tests are easy to repeat.

1 Raw materials may be tested when they are brought into the factory. Examples include:
- checking the colour of crumb to be used to coat fish fingers
- checking the amount of acid in milk coming from a farm into a dairy.

2 Many companies require their suppliers to provide a certificate with each delivery, giving details about the material supplied. This avoids the need to test every delivery. This system is essential for manufacturers using just in time (JIT) deliveries.

3 Equipment used in manufacturing and testing must be checked regularly to make sure it is working accurately. Examples include:
- checking that the temperature inside an oven is the same as that set on the dial
- checking that a timer used to time a process is working accurately.

4 Tests carried out during food manufacture make use of feedback to ensure that any faults can be quickly put right. This minimises waste from faulty finished products. Examples include:
- checking the weight of dough being used to make a loaf of bread
- checking the temperature of chocolate being used to enrobe chocolate biscuits.

5 Some quality control (QC) tests are carried out on finished products. Tests for each product are listed in the product specification along with the tolerance for the test results.

Examples of sensory tests include:
- the colour of baked pastry
- the texture of pasta (cooked before testing)
- the taste of fish fingers (cooked before testing).

Examples of physical and chemical tests include:
- measuring that loaves of bread have risen to the correct height
- analysing the amount of salt present in potato crisps.

In your coursework project you will need to:

- design and use quality checks to test the fitness for purpose of your product
- check the quality of your product at appropriate points in its manufacture
- test your product to make sure it complies with your product specification
- suggest ways of improving the quality of your product.

Examples of microbiological tests include:

- testing products such as chicken portions, cream cakes, fresh pasta and quiches to make sure that they will not spoil
- testing to make sure that the products are not a risk to **consumer** health.

> **Coursework checkpoint: *testing***
>
> ○ Products need to be tested before and during manufacture to save time and costly mistakes later on.
>
> Design a series of tests that are linked to your product specification. This will help you produce a high quality, value-for-money food product. The tests you use will depend upon the type of product you are making, but might include:
>
> ○ weight and quality of the ingredients
> ○ product appearance
> ○ sensory quality
> ○ nett weight.

the **texture** of food describes the sensation it gives when you bite into it and take it into your mouth. Words that are used to describe the texture of foods include:

- hard
- soft
- crumbly
- chewy
- bitty
- slimy
- gooey
- gummy
- sticky
- tender
- tough
- crunchy
- light
- fluffy
- heavy
- dry
- moist
- watery
- greasy.

The texture of food changes during manufacturing processes, due to changes in the food materials. For example:

- water is lost by evaporation during baking – the food becomes dryer
- **proteins** in **egg** may form a foam through beating – the food becomes much 'lighter' due to the increase in volume.

thickeners are **additives** and are given E numbers. Thickeners are similar to some **stabilisers** because they are able to bind large quantities of water. Some substances such as Xanthan gum can be used as *either* thickeners *or* as stabilisers. Thickeners can be used, for example:

- to increase the viscosity of sauces, so that they can coat food more readily
- in soups to give them more 'body'
- in fruit pies, to prevent liquid in the fruit from soaking into the **pastry**.

Starch (cornflour) is the most commonly used thickener in home cooking and is also widely used in industry.

Name of thickener	E number	Examples of products they are used in
Sodium carboxy methyl cellulose and carrageenan	E466 E407	Custard
Gum Arabic	E414	Chewing gum
Locust bean gum and Xanthan gum	E410 E415	Fruit snack drink
Xanthan gum	E415	Dessert sauces

Table 19 Examples of thickeners and the products they are used in

Coursework checkpoint: *thickeners*

Investigate the effect of thickeners by making up a roux recipe, first of all using plain **flour**, and then make it again using cornflour. You can also try using different amounts of flour or cornflour (but use the same amount of liquid each time).

tolerances are needed when setting target values for quality indicators in a food product specification. There is always some variability within a batch of products or during an hour's production on a continuous production line. This is unavoidable because food ingredients are natural materials that will vary. The manufacturer must decide how far the product may move from a target value before the quality of the food is affected.

1. Tolerances are easy to set for variables. For example, if biscuits should have a diameter of 5.0cm, then this is the target value.
   - If the diameter is more than 5.2cm, the biscuits may not fit in the packaging.
   - If the diameter is less than 4.8cm, the biscuits might look smaller than the consumer expects them to be.

   The specification will need to state that the diameter of the biscuits has a target value of 5.0cm with a tolerance of +/- 0.2cm.

2. Tolerances can also be set for attributes. These are quality indicators that cannot be directly measured, such as pie crust colour.

- The product specification might describe the target colour as an 'attractive golden-brown'.
- A photograph of a pie with the target crust colour would be included in the product specification. Photographs of a pale crust pie and a dark crust pie would also be included to show the allowable colour tolerances.
- Photographs of pies with acceptable crust colours would be kept for reference by the production line to make sure that the colour tolerances were not exceeded.

a **trade mark** (brand name, trade name) is used by manufacturers to protect and promote a food product so that it can't be legally copied by competitors.

In your coursework project you will need to:

- take account of critical dimensions when planning the manufacture of your product
- work out the degree of accuracy needed for your product to function as planned
- take account of tolerance when planning your product manufacture so that your product meets its specification.

trend-forecasting is an essential activity for **product development teams**, for production management and for supermarket managers. Food fashions are influenced by:

- cookery programmes
- foreign travel
- food 'scares', putting people off particular foods
- the weather.

Market research can help to discover some trends, but flexibility in food product development and manufacture and in the management of supermarket retail space is important to ensure that **consumers** can always find the foods they want.

u

Ultra High Temperature (UHT) is a heat **sterilisation** process carried out at temperatures generally in excess of 140°C. UHT is a very rapid process because the temperature is so high. Changes to the sensory and nutritional quality of the food are much less than in conventional sterilisation. UHT processing is used for some types of milk and for some soups. Unlike pasteurised milk, UHT milk can be kept at **ambient** temperature and has a **shelf life** of six months.

unit operations are processes used in food manufacture, such as:

- **cleaning** (removal of physical contaminants from the food)
- peeling
- **mixing** (blending different ingredients together)
- **size reduction** (making food pieces smaller in some way)
- **heat processing** (pasteurisation, canning, sterilisation, Ultra High Temperature (UHT) processing, baking, boiling, frying, roasting)
- freezing
- drying.

> **In your coursework project you will need to:**
> - identify the unit operations that can be linked together to make your own product.

The following example shows how unit operations are linked together to make mashed potatoes:

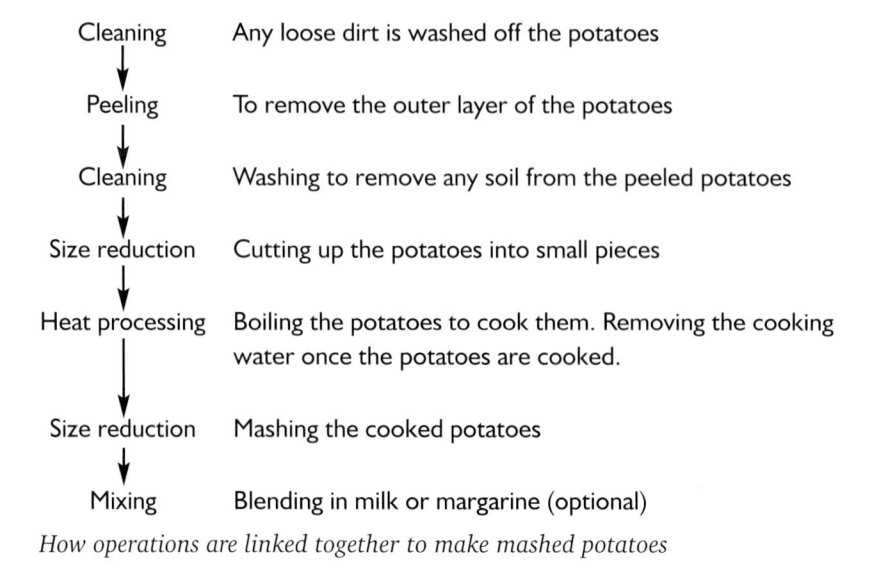

Cleaning	Any loose dirt is washed off the potatoes
↓	
Peeling	To remove the outer layer of the potatoes
↓	
Cleaning	Washing to remove any soil from the peeled potatoes
↓	
Size reduction	Cutting up the potatoes into small pieces
↓	
Heat processing	Boiling the potatoes to cook them. Removing the cooking water once the potatoes are cooked.
↓	
Size reduction	Mashing the cooked potatoes
↓	
Mixing	Blending in milk or margarine (optional)

How operations are linked together to make mashed potatoes

These unit operations come within the processing, **assembly** and finishing sections of the **stages of production**.

> **Coursework checkpoint:** *unit operations*
>
> Draw up a table to show the unit operations involved in making each of the following food products:
> - Beefburger.
> - Fruit pie.
> - Sponge cake.

user trials are carried out by some food **manufacturers** during product development (PD). Members of the public are asked to **taste** a product and give their views on it. This can be done by sending the product to people's homes or by stopping them in a shopping mall and asking them to taste the product. **Feedback** from user trials is used to modify, where necessary, the design or manufacture of the product, so it meets **consumer** requirements more closely.

In your coursework project you will need to:

- use tests, modifications and evaluation to ensure that your food product matches your **product** and **manufacturing process specifications**.

> **Coursework checkpoint:** *user trials*
>
> You can use a user trial to provide valuable feedback about your product's performance in use. It can form part of your product evaluation.

values issues must be considered by any **manufacturer** wishing to develop and manufacture food products. Values issues include:
- food safety
- ensuring the production of nutritious food
- environmental issues.

All of these issues are covered by **legislation**. The food industry is subject to more regulations than any other in this country. Most regulations are enacted under the Food Safety Act (1990).

The food industry also has to allow for issues that concern specific groups of **consumers**, such as labelling foods to alert consumers who may suffer from allergies. Many manufacturers are also reducing levels of salt and saturated **fats** in their products, as a response to government concerns over obesity and heart disease in this country.

The market for **organic foods** is growing, as consumers become more concerned about the effects of **additives** used in food processing and the use of chemicals in food production. The demand for vegetarian foods is strong, particularly among younger people. Cultural, ethnic and religious preferences must also be considered, in order to fulfil a market demand without causing offence to consumers.

Moral issues that have to be addressed include attitudes to factory farming, the management of **genetically modified (GM)** food development and the need for farmers in poorer countries to receive a fair price for their products.

In your coursework project you will need to:

- make good use of social, cultural and environmental influences when developing product ideas.

> **Coursework checkpoint:** *values issues*
>
> Use the Internet and any other available sources of information to investigate the work and aims of the Fair Trade organisation in food production and marketing.

Understanding Industrial Practices: Food Technology © Nelson Thornes 2005

vitamins are required in small quantities and are essential for health. They must be supplied in the human diet as they cannot be made in the body.

The way vitamins react to different types of processing affects the nutritional value of foods. Although vitamins are lost during processing, a balanced diet normally contains sufficient vitamins for

	Vitamin A (retinol)	**Vitamin B1 (thiamin)**	**Vitamin B2 (riboflavin)**	**Vitamin C (ascorbic acid)**	**Vitamin D**
Solubility	Fat soluble	Water soluble	Water soluble	Water soluble	Fat soluble
Main food sources	Orange-coloured pigments in fruits and vegetables are converted into vitamin A in the human body	Bread and other cereal foods. Milk, meat and potatoes.	Milk, cereal foods, liver and eggs	Fruits and vegetables, (especially fresh or frozen). Loss of vitamin C occurs in stored fruits and vegetables.	Oily fish, such as mackerel and salmon. Butter, cheese and margarine.
Effects of processing	Very stable during processing or cooking	Breaks down with heat. Heavy losses during processing or cooking. Some is lost if the cooking water is thrown away.	Only small losses during processing or cooking. Will break down in sunlight, e.g. if milk bottles are left on a doorstep.	Heavy losses during processing or cooking and by throwing away cooking water. Steaming vegetables (instead of boiling) will help to retain vitamin C.	Very stable during processing or cooking

Table 20 Vitamins

Key people

The **key people** involved in the production process include:

- clients (customers)
- marketing people who check out what will sell, to whom and at what price
- product developers (designers)
- technologists
- manufacturers
- retailers (who may be the client)
- consumers.

The **client** (customer) is a person or organisation that asks for a product to be designed and manufactured. This is often the manufacturer or retailer of the product. The role of the client is to:

- identify a need or opportunity for manufacturing a product
- organise key people to get the product manufactured and to the market
- agree a brief with the designer or design team
- agree a budget and raise money for the project
- agree a time-plan and deadlines for production.

The **product development manager** will work with a team to incorporate sensory and aesthetic appeal, nutritional value, low cost, safety and sales appeal in a finished product. Members of the product development team may take on more than one role, such as marketing or technologist. The role of the product development manager is to:

- agree a design brief with the client (customer)
- check that an identified need is realistic and viable
- investigate specifications for existing company products
- agree with the client the design specification criteria
- take account of legislation and design safe products
- produce original product ideas based on the design specification and available budget
- consider environmental, social and moral implications of their product ideas
- suggest materials and production techniques.

Technologists plan the manufacture of the product at the highest quality and lowest cost.

Food technologists make sure that safe food products are made using the most appropriate production methods. The role of the technologist is to:

- produce costings for the product
- evaluate product prototypes for quality, cost and availability of ingredients
- organise sensory evaluation of products for consumer acceptability
- develop manufacturing process specifications, details of materials, components and manufacturing processes
- monitor quality in production.

Manufacturers need to make a profit otherwise the company will go out of business. They employ key people in the production team to design and manufacture the product. The role of manufacturers is to:

- be aware of the target market needs
- produce a production plan
- set up a cost-effective manufacturing system that can meet demand
- plan for ease of manufacture, reduce material and labour costs so they make a profit
- produce consistent products using a quality assurance (QA) system
- manufacture products that are safe for employees, consumers and the environment.

Consumers are the people all products are aimed at. Their needs are very important if manufacturers and retailers are to make a profit. A lot of effort goes into finding out what consumers really want or will buy. Most consumers demand:

- products that are safe to use and that meet current consumer legislation
- products that are fit for their intended purpose and that meet expectations of nutritional quality
- products that reflect current lifestyle trends, e.g. ethnic foods, low-fat foods
- value for money products that have an acceptable quality.

Coursework checklists

1 How to manage your coursework project

- Find out the project deadline so you know how many weeks you have for your coursework.
- Read the assessment criteria so you know how many marks are available for research, design, manufacture and evaluation.
- Find out the number of pages you need to have in your project folder.
- Too much research is a waste of time. Ask your teacher how much research you should do.
- Tick off your teacher's checklist as you work through your project.
- Try grading your own project against the assessment criteria.

2 What to include in your coursework project folder

When designing you should include:

- a **design brief**, stating the type and purpose of the product you will design and the **target market** it is aimed at
- an analysis of the design brief resulting in a list of what you need to research. Check your research list with your teacher.
- an analysis and summary of your research into similar commercial products, the needs and **values** of the target market, food fashion trends, ingredients, processes, nutritional requirements, value for money, **quality** and safety
- only information that is relevant to the development of your product. Check your analysis and research with your teacher.
- a **design specification** that sets out detailed criteria about the product you will design. Make sure that you use your design specification to guide your design ideas.
- a brainstorm or mind map to explore and explain your first ideas about your product. Use this as a starting point for generating design proposals.
- design proposals that are evaluated against your design specification criteria
- a design solution that is developed from your design proposals. Your design solution should meet your design specification criteria.

When **modelling, prototyping, planning** production and manufacturing you should include:

- clear evidence of modelling, prototyping and **testing** your design solution. Allow enough time to evaluate your work as it progresses. Modify your design solution if necessary. Record and explain any changes.
- a **product specification, manufacturing process specification, production plan** and **schedule for manufacture** that details how to manufacture one product and how it could be manufactured in quantity
- clear evidence of the safe manufacture of a high **quality** product that meets your design and manufacturing criteria
- evidence of evaluation against **specifications** throughout the design and manufacturing process. Compare the product with a similar commercial one and record the views of the **target market**. Suggest how to improve the market potential of your product.

3 How to show evidence of industrial practices in your coursework

- Use **key words** (see page 91) to help you use technical terms like those used in industry.
- Use the A–Z and worksheets to help you use designing activities like those used in industry.
- Use the A–Z and worksheets to help you use manufacturing activities like those used in industry.

4 How to use ICT in your coursework

- List how you will use **Information and Communication Technology (ICT)** and **computer-aided design (CAD)** for research, designing, **modelling**, communicating and testing.
- At the start of your project, make a list of how you will use ICT and **computer-aided manufacture (CAM)** for analysing information, production planning and manufacture.

5 How to use systems and control in your coursework

- Plan how you will use a **computer system** to control the design and manufacture of your product.
- Plan how you will use a **quality control (QC)** system that incorporates **feedback** to help you manufacture a high **quality** product.
- Plan how you could use a safety system.

Key words

Context for design
- Design brief, problem, consumer needs and wants, market opportunities, scale of production.
- Target market group, clients, product developers, manufacturers, retailers, consumers.

Research
- Product analysis, aesthetics, eating trends, market research, trend-forecasting, product cost and quality.
- Target market group, consumer needs and wants, lifestyle, product size/weight, environmental issues, recycling, values issues.
- Availability of ingredients, standard components, processes, equipment, health & safety (H&S).
- Internet, ICT, questionnaire, shop report.

Analysis
- Analysis, conclusions and summary of research.

Design specification
- Design specification, design criteria.
- Product end-use, function or purpose.
- Product consumers, target market group.
- Aesthetics, consumer method of use, availability of materials, standard components, product size/weight, packaging, processes, scale of production, cost.
- Quality requirements, brand, cost limits.
- Safety requirements, labels, legislation, shelf life.
- Environmental and values issues.

Design ideas
- Brainstorm, mind map.
- First ideas, creative, design proposals, evaluation against design specification criteria.

Design development
- Design solution, ingredients, aesthetic values, nutritional values, processes, CAD, evaluation against design specification criteria, shelf life testing, modification of solution.

Materials
- Fresh ingredients, composite products, standard components, packaging materials.
- Aesthetic and functional properties of ingredients:
  - Colour, flavour, texture.
  - Binding, emulsifying, setting, stabilising, thickening.

Modelling and prototyping
- CAD, 2D modelling, 3D prototyping, testing, ingredients, processes, costing, spreadsheet.
- Time to evaluate, modify, fitness for purpose, record and explain changes.

Planning production
- Designing for manufacture, CAD, product specification, production plan, manufacturing process specification, schedule for manufacture, recipe, quality assurance (QA), tolerance, product size/weight.
- Gantt chart, flow chart, input-process-output, quality control (QC), critical control point (CCP), feedback, health & safety (H&S), risk assessment, hazards.
- Production system, computer system, control system, QA, safety system, risk assessment, method of production, one-off, batch production, mass production, continuous production, automation, computer integrated manufacturing (CIM).

Manufacturing
- Recipe, ingredients, equipment, packaging materials, processes, times, temperatures, critical control points (CCPs), testing, target values and tolerances, computer-aided design (CAD), costing.
- Computer-aided manufacture (CAM), processing equipment.
- Stages of production, product specification, manufacturing process specification, preparation, processing, assembly, finishing, packaging, storage.

Machines and processes
- Mixers, scales, pans, oven, chiller, freezer, time, temperature.
- Finishing techniques, CAD/CAM.

Evaluation and testing
- Quality control (QC), critical control point (CCP), quality indicators, feedback, inspection, specifications, target values and tolerances, fitness for purpose.
- Target market group, sensory analysis, user trial, feedback.
- Modifications, improvements, marketing.

1 batch production

Name ....

Form/group .... **Date** ....

Working as a team, design and make a batch of cookies that could be made quickly and efficiently and sold in school. Your recipe and any decoration must be simple so that the cookies are easy to make.

You will need to:
- set up a design and production team of 4–6 students
- allocate and agree each team member's role using the following list of design and manufacturing activities.

Design and manufacturing activities

1. The whole team carries out **market research** to find the **consumers'** preferences for types of cookies and decoration. (You could investigate different recipes, shapes, **colours** and types of decoration.)
2. Work as a team to agree a **design specification** for your product.
3. Work in your agreed roles to manufacture a small **prototype batch** of cookies to test your design, organisational skills and manufacturing abilities.

Job descriptions
- The production manager works out the easiest way to make the batch of cookies, checks the availability of materials and equipment and carries out the **costing** for the product. The product selling price needs to be attractive to the consumer and make a profit.
- The quality controller (QC) identifies where, and how, to check for **quality** ensuring each product is satisfactory. The QC checks quality during manufacture and runs a final quality check before the product is passed for sale. (Remember to build **tolerance** into your **quality indicators**, your products will not all be identical.)
- The production operatives are responsible for weighing, **mixing**, forming the cookies, baking, cooling and decorating.

Team role	Name of student
Market research	
Produce design specification	
Production manager	
Quality controller	
Weighing/baking *	
Mixing/cooling *	
Forming cookies/decorating *	

(*These operations can be separated or combined, depending on the number of team members.)

Further work

1. Use **feedback** from the prototype batch of cookies to make any modifications necessary to improve your design specification.
2. Evaluate how successful your team was in designing and manufacturing the cookies. Was each cookie of satisfactory quality? If not, what further improvements could you make to your recipe or your way of working?
3. Evaluate how well each team member worked. Did anyone have too much/not enough to do?
4. Plan how you will market your cookies. Will the selling price be attractive to consumers? How will you advertise and display your product?

2   colour

Name ....

Form/group .... **Date** ....

Using **colour** to make food more attractive to the **consumer** is very important to anyone concerned in **product development (PD)** and the **marketing** of food.

1. Using the table below, make a list of vegetables that could be eaten raw with a dip.

Vegetable	Raw colour	Colour effect on a vegetable platter (✓ or ✗)

2. Design a platter of raw vegetables to accompany a range of dips that could form an attractive feature on a buffet table at a birthday party. If you wish, you can use a garnish as a **finishing process** to add to the attractiveness of your platter.

3. Sketch in colour the layout of your platter, to show how you have used vegetable colour to attract the consumers.

4. Describe the **cleaning** and **size reduction** processes you would use to make the vegetables suitable for their intended use.

Further work

Write a description of the desired colour of a **pastry** topping on a fruit pie that could form part of a **product specification**. How could you make this colour and colour **tolerance** limits easy to understand for people making the pies?

3 using CAD

You have been commissioned to produce the cover for a menu for the Hearty Foods Restaurant. The restaurant wants to promote its pasta dishes so you should include a picture of a pasta-based dish in your design.

You should work in teams for this task.

1 Each team member should look for pictures of pasta dishes on plates. Examine food magazines; recipe books; websites; and serving suggestions on ready-meal **packaging**.

2 In your team, use the information you have gained to answer the following questions:
   - How has **colour** been used to make the food look attractive?
   - What ingredients have been used to give an attractive **appearance** to the food?
   - How has the food been arranged to improve the **aesthetic quality** of the picture? Have any props been used (e.g. a tablecloth, knife and fork, or a glass of water)?
   - What **finishing processes** have been used (e.g. using a piece of tomato or a sprig of parsley as a garnish)?

3 As a team, decide what to put in your picture. Assemble the materials and props needed. You will have to cook some pasta. Other ingredients may (or may not) need to be cooked.

4 Take some photographs of your pasta dish. Use a **computer-aided design (CAD)** programme to incorporate the best photo and the name of the restaurant into a cover design for the menu.

4 computer systems

Name ....

Form/group .... **Date** ....

Computer systems play an important role in the food industry.

1. Give three examples of the general use of computer systems in the food industry.

2. Give three examples of the use of specialist computer systems in food manufacturing.

3. Describe the benefits to food **manufacturers** of using computer systems.

4. Using the input-process-output diagrams below, explain how you could use a computer system to help you:
   a) model design ideas for a food **packaging label**
   b) mix a batch of dough for making bread
   c) fill bottles of tomato ketchup with the same weight of ketchup every time.

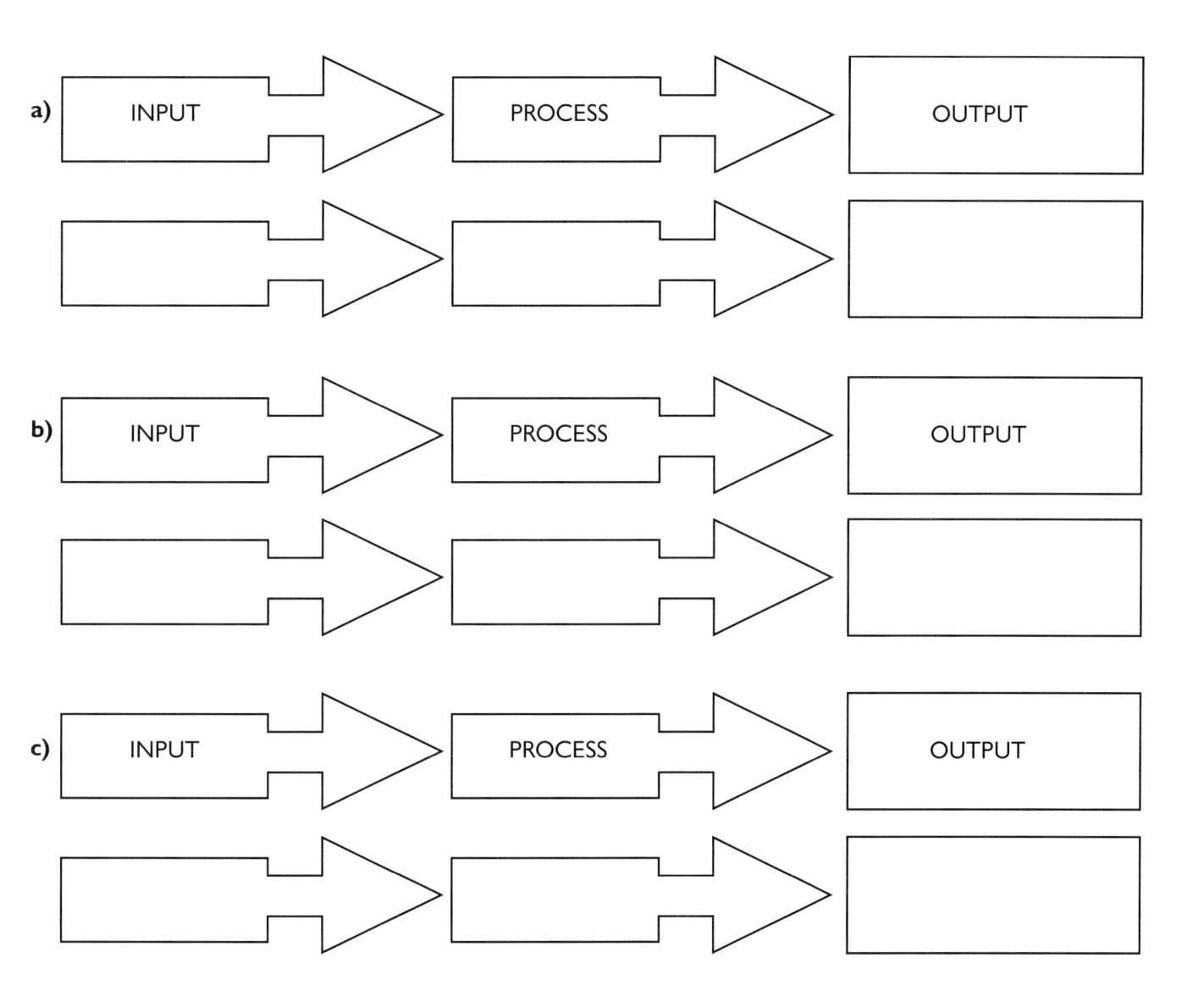

a) INPUT → PROCESS → OUTPUT

b) INPUT → PROCESS → OUTPUT

c) INPUT → PROCESS → OUTPUT

5 continuous production

Name ....

Form/group .... **Date** ....

1. Give three examples of food products manufactured using **continuous production** techniques. Explain why they are made using this **method of production**.

2. Explain why a food **production line** used for continuous production must be shut down at regular intervals.

3. Give three reasons why **custom-made** food products are more expensive to buy than those made by continuous production.

4. Describe two benefits of using sensors to monitor continuous production machinery.

5. Describe the differences between **batch production**, **high-volume production** and continuous production.

6 control systems

Name ....

Form/group .... Date ....

A computerised **control system** can be used to package different varieties of crisps and choose the number of packets of each variety to be placed into multipacks.

Block diagrams are used in control systems to show how inputs are processed to achieve outputs.

1 Draw a block diagram to show an open loop system for placing two packets of each of three different varieties into a multipack of crisps.

2 Decide how **feedback** could be used to ensure the correct varieties of crisps are placed in the multipacks and draw a closed loop system to show where this feedback occurs.

Further work

Draw a block diagram to show how you could undertake each of the following activities:

    a) Use a food mixer to make a cake batter.

    b) Use an automatic bread making machine.

    c) Help design your product.

7 costing

Name ....

Form/group .... Date ....

A delicatessen has asked you to supply 50 mushroom and onion quiches per week. These are made at your factory in batches of 100 and costs are calculated per 100. You need to estimate your selling price for the 50 quiches to be sure the delicatessen will place an order. Work out your **costing** in the set stages shown below.

a) Work out the Direct Costs for the 50 quiches.
   Ingredients
   Pastry @ £13.00 per 100 quiches   =
   Filling (mushrooms, onions, eggs, seasoning)
      @ £58.00 per 100 quiches   =
   Packaging (foil dish + cardboard box)
      @ £6.80 per 100 quiches   =
   Labour
   2 hours @ £6.20 per hour   =
   Total Direct Costs   =

b) Work out the Overhead Costs for the 50 quiches.
   The Overhead Cost   = 40% of the labour cost
                                                    =

c) Work out the Manufacturing Costs for the 50 quiches.
   Manufacturing Costs   = Direct Costs + Overhead Costs
                                                    =
                                                    =

d) Work out the Manufacturing Profit for the 50 quiches.
   Manufacturing Profit   = 60% of the Manufacturing Costs
                                                    =

e) Work out the Selling Price for the 50 quiches.
   Selling Price   = Manufacturing Costs + Manufacturing Profit
                                                    =
                                                    =

Further work

1. The delicatessen may say that the price is too high. Work out how you can reduce the price to make sure of the order. Remember that:
   - this customer wants half a batch of quiches; cheaper ingredients could upset your other customers
   - quiches are a **high-risk** product with a short **shelf life**. Your customer will not be able to increase the order unless their sales increase.

2. You will need to accurately work out costs for your own product, so don't just guess. Remember to include all the ingredients and **packaging** costs, labour costs and overhead costs, such as rent and electricity (or gas) for cooking and food storage. The selling price of your product must be attractive to your **target market group**, as well as making you a profit.
   - Negotiate an overhead percentage with your teacher, based on the rent of the kitchen, energy costs, and use of the equipment.
   - No one is 100% efficient, so make allowances for this by adding a small percentage to your labour charge, such as 5%.

8 critical control points

In the food industry **critical control points (CCPs)** are used to ensure that food poses no risk to the health of the **consumer**.

1 Read the following account of the stages in the production of roast turkey for serving as a roast lunch.

The turkey has been stored in a freezer, as **bacteria** will not grow at −18°C. Two days before it is to be cooked, the turkey is moved into a fridge. The turkey then thaws at a low temperature that restricts the growth of bacteria. If the turkey is not completely thawed when it goes into the oven it may not cook completely and some bacteria will not be destroyed.

The turkey is roasted in the oven. If the oven is not hot enough, or the cooking time is too short, some bacteria may not be destroyed.

The turkey is taken from the oven and left for a few minutes to draw the juices back into the meat. Slices of meat are carved off. If the knife is not completely clean, or the person doing the carving has not got clean hands, then bacteria may be transferred on to the turkey.

After carving, the remainder of the turkey is left to cool. Once its temperature drops below 63°C any bacteria may start to grow, so it is important that the turkey is transferred to the fridge as soon as it is cool enough.

2 Using the information above, draw a **Hazard Analysis Critical Control Point (HACCP) flow chart**, similar to the one in worksheet 17. Decide which stages in the production of roast turkey are CCPs. Describe the controls and monitoring procedures you would put in place at each CCP.

9 custom-made product

Your **design brief** is to make and decorate a sponge cake to celebrate a special occasion for a family member or a friend. Before you can make your cake you need to be sure it will fulfil your customer's requirements. Remember that your customer is the person who is asking you to make the cake; not necessarily the person it is being made for, especially if it is being made as a surprise gift.

Write a **design specification** and include a file of ideas and information you can show to your customer to help them choose a design. Find out the cost of ingredients, including bought-in ribbon and decorations for the top and a board to put the cake on. Include prices for different finished designs in your file. You can use the **costing** worksheet (worksheet 7) to help you work out the cost of your cake.

You will need to include information about:

- the shape and size of cake that you can make. (If you have only one set of cake tins there will not be any choice, but your customer will still need to know the shape and size.)
- **flavours** available for the sponge (e.g. lemon, chocolate, coffee)
- fillings available (e.g. strawberry or seedless raspberry jam, chocolate buttercream)
- **finishing processes** available. Normally a celebration cake is iced, but this is not essential. Include some sketches of ways to decorate the top and maybe the sides of your cake.

You must consult with your customer and agree the final design, price and date of delivery.

Once you have this information, place an order for the materials you need, so that they are ready when you need them.

Make and decorate your cake. You must allow time for this, but remember sponge cakes will dry out, so ideally make and decorate the cake the day before it is needed.

2 Explain why it is important that celebration cakes should be made as **custom-made** products.

3 Explain the advantages and disadvantages to the **manufacturer** of making custom-made products.

10 writing a design brief

Name ....

Form/group .... Date ....

You have been commissioned by a local café to develop a range of snack bar products, with a low fat and low sugar content. If your snack bars are approved you may be asked to produce them in quantity. You will need to develop two different snack bars, and list different **flavours** that each could be produced in.

Write a **design brief** to describe:

- the type of products you will develop, such as a cake bar, fruit and cereal bar or biscuit, their approximate size and weight

- the **target market group** – who would buy your products. Who uses the café; what age group should your products appeal to; should they appeal equally to men and women?

- the purpose of the products, such as a snack to eat with a cup of tea or coffee, or something to provide a light substitute for lunch.

Further work

Research the requirements of young people buying take-away foods. Take into account when and where these foods are bought and the acceptable price to be paid.

Write a design brief to describe:

- the type of product you will design

- the target market group

- the end use of the product.

11 writing a design specification

You have been commissioned by a local community café to develop a nutritious soup for elderly people. Write a **design specification** for the soup, using the following questions to guide your thinking.

- What is the purpose of the product?

- Will it be made as a **one-off, batch** or **high-volume** product?

- What is the **target market group**? What is their age range? What special nutritional needs do they have?

- What should the product look like?

- What ingredients are readily available and suitable for the product?

- What **flavours** and **textures** of ingredients would be attractive?

- How much will the **consumer** be prepared to pay?

- What is the price range of similar products on the market?

- How will the product be prepared for consumption?

- What size/weight of packs would be suitable for your customer?

- What **shelf life** will your product have?

Further work

- Use your design specification to help you develop two recipes for soups.

- Add notes to explain the ingredients you have chosen to use.

- Explain how your products will fulfil the requirements of your design specification.

- Design a name and 'serving suggestion' picture for the **label** of your product.

- When you write a design specification for your own product, remember to include the deadlines for developing and making your product.

12   designing for manufacture

You have been commissioned by your local delicatessen to develop a fresh, chilled sauce that could accompany pasta. The delicatessen wants the sauce to be delivered in 5kg plastic tubs, so that they can put it into small pots for their customers. Your sauce must be suitable for vegetarians.

Market research has indicated that a tomato-based sauce containing chopped onions and red and green peppers would be popular.

1. Write a description of the product. Consider, for example, what **colour** and how thick the sauce should be; what size should the pieces of onion and peppers be; should the tomato seeds be removed?

2. How will you manufacture the sauce: as a **one-off, batch** or **high-volume** product?

3. What ingredients will you need? Which ingredients can be bought-in as **standard components**?

4. What processes will be needed to make your sauce? List the equipment and tools that will be needed. Note any training that will be required to gain the skills needed to operate any of the equipment.

5. What steps will you take to ensure that **food safety** is assured?

6. What steps will you take to ensure that a high **quality** product is made?

Further work

Use the information you have gained to write out a **manufacturing process specification** for the sauce.

13   feedback

Name ....

Form/group .... **Date** ....

Your **product development team** has carried out a **user trial** of a new pour-over sauce to be used with ice-cream. 50 families were given unlabelled bottles of the sauce and asked to comment on how much they liked it, using a scale of 1 to 5. They were also asked for comments on the sauce.

1 = dislike a lot
2 = dislike a bit
3 = neither like nor dislike
4 = like a little
5 = like a lot

The table below shows the number of families that gave each score.

Score	1	2	3	4	5
Number of responses	4	10	18	12	6

Some typical comments received about the sauce:
- 'Delicious – the whole family loved it, and it didn't stick to the ice-cream like glue, like some products do.'
- 'Not sweet enough – the kids didn't like it.'
- 'Really fruity and not too sweet – my husband and I loved it.'
- 'Our family didn't like it as much as our normal brand, we thought it was too runny and the taste was too sharp.'
- 'I expected it to be really sweet, but it wasn't; I could still taste the ice-cream, and I liked that.'
- 'I only ever buy this type of product for the kids, they thought it was OK but prefer their usual brand as the fruit isn't so strong in that.'

Analyse the information you have gained to provide **feedback** to the product development team.

Consider the following:
- What was most liked about the sauce?
- What was least liked about the sauce?
- Who is likely to be the **target market group** for this product?
- Sketch an idea for a picture to go on the **label** that would appeal to the target market group.

Using all the information, make a recommendation to the product development team. Should they go ahead and launch this product, or should they scrap it because it is unlikely to sell enough to make a profit? Give reasons to support your decision.

14 flow chart

Flow chart symbols

○   An operation is performed on the food material.

□   An inspection (or test) is made on the food material.

▽   The food is stored.

D   Delay. The food is kept in one place for a period of time.

⇨   The food is transported from one place to another.

1. Using the **flow chart** symbols above, draw a flow chart to show the stages in making a sponge cake.

2. Mark on the chart where you would carry out **quality control (QC)** checks to ensure you make a high **quality** product.

3. Where appropriate, incorporate **feedback** loops into your flow chart to show how you would use your QC data.

Further work

Include a flow chart in the **manufacturing process specification** for your product.

15   food safety

Name ....

Form/group .... Date ....

It is most important to make sure that any food you make will not cause any harm to anyone who eats it. In your coursework project you will be expected to take responsibility for making sure that your product is made and stored safely.

1. Explain what is meant by the **shelf life** of a food.

2. Describe three steps that food **manufacturers** must take to make sure that the food they produce is safe for **consumers**.

3. Describe three steps that food retailers must take to make sure that the food they sell is always safe for consumers.

4. Describe two **quality control (QC)** checks that you can carry out to make sure the foods in the refrigerator in your school kitchen are safe to eat.

16   hazard analysis

Name ....

Form/group... Date ....

1. Describe three **hazards** to operator safety in your school kitchen.

2. Explain the steps taken in the kitchen to minimise the risk associated with each hazard you have listed.

3. Explain how a **high-risk** area in a food factory can be used to control hazards that might be associated with some foods.

4. Look at the picture of part of a food **label** below. Explain the hazards that the **manufacturer** is attempting to control through the information being given to the **consumer**.

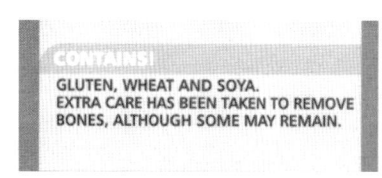

Further work

Carry out a **hazard analysis** for the manufacture and consumption of your product to make sure any hazards associated with your product are being controlled.

Write down:

    a) any precautions that need to be taken during manufacture

    b) any information that needs to be given to the consumer.

Understanding Industrial Practices: Food Technology © Nelson Thornes 2005

17 hazard analysis critical control point

Hazard Analysis Critical Control Point (HACCP) is used in food factories and in the catering industry to look at the potential **hazards** in a food operation. A HACCP team is always used to set up a HACCP **system** because several people are always better at seeing all the potential problems (hazards) than just one person.

What to do:

1. Study the HACCP diagram below for producing a homemade beefburger. This is a **high-risk** food product. This means that **bacteria** can easily grow in it, so that it could spoil, or cause food-poisoning if it is not treated properly.

Flow chart	Hazard	Is it a CCP?	Control measure	Monitoring procedure
Weigh ingredients (minced beef, chopped onion and breadcrumbs)	Scales and kitchen tools not properly cleaned	**Yes** (unclean equipment may transfer bacteria to burger)	Make sure all equipment is properly cleaned	Check all equipment before use
Mix ingredients, using a food mixer, or hands	Hands (or food mixer) not clean	**Yes** (unclean hands or mixer can transfer bacteria to burger)	Make sure mixer is properly cleaned and hands washed thoroughly	Visual check
Form burger, by hand, or using a burger press	Hands (or burger press) not clean	**Yes** (unclean hands or burger press can transfer bacteria to burger)	Make sure press is properly cleaned and hands washed thoroughly	Visual check
Store burger in fridge	Fridge temp. too high and/or burger kept too long	**Yes** (high temp. and/or long storage let bacteria grow)	Make sure fridge temp. is below 5°C; burger used within 24 hours	Keep record of fridge temp. Note date burger is put in fridge – throw out if not used.
Grill or fry burger	Burger not fully cooked	**Yes** (bacteria may survive in under-cooked food)	Make sure burger is cooked right through	Cut a burger in two to check cooked appearance. Note cooking time and heat setting.
Serve burger for student tea	Student not ready for tea	**No**		

2. Select your HACCP team.

3. Devise a HACCP diagram for one of the following:
   a) Making a boiled egg.
   b) Making a ham sandwich.

18 high volume production (1)

Read through the following description of how bread is manufactured in a large bakery.

Making the dough

- **Flour**, yeast (supplied as a suspension called a slurry) and cold water are metered into a large mixer. Other ingredients, **fat** and salt, are weighed and added to the mixer by hand. The next person to handle any of the mixer contents will be the **consumer** who opens up the loaf of bread!
- A bakery worker closes a gate so that no one can touch the mixer while it is running, then presses a switch on a control panel to start the mixer.
- When the dough is mixed, the mixer empties automatically and the dough is cut into pieces weighing about 860g (for large bread loaves).

The dough becomes bread

- The dough pieces are rounded into balls. After 10 minutes each ball is rolled out into a 'swiss-roll' shape and dropped into a bread tin.
- The tins move on a conveyor into a prover machine, where they are warmed to 40°C. Moist air prevents a skin forming on the dough. After 45 minutes, the dough has more than doubled its height, due to the action of the yeast.
- The tins travel slowly on a conveyor belt through a long tunnel oven, which is designed for **continuous, high volume production**. Baking time is set by controlling the speed of the conveyor through the oven, which has heaters along its length and an opening at each end.

After baking

- As the loaves leave the oven they are lifted from the tins by suction.
- The loaves are cooled down to room temperature, sliced and bagged.
- The bags are sealed with a piece of tape that has the 'best before' date written on it.

What to do:
Study the list below, which gives the stages in bread manufacture. Place the stages in the order they occur during the manufacturing process.

Bagging the bread
Baking
Cooling
Dividing the dough
De-panning (removing the loaves from the tins)
Mixing
Proving
Rolling out the dough
Rounding the dough into balls
Sealing the bags
Slicing the bread
Transferring the dough into tins

19 high volume production (2)

Name ....

Form/group.. Date ....

Read the description on worksheet 18 of how bread is manufactured.

Now answer the following questions about the bread making process.

1. Give an example of a **health and safety (H&S)** procedure mentioned in the description of bread manufacture.

2. State which part of the manufacturing process is not controlled by computer.

3. State which ingredient is responsible for the bread dough rising during proving. What is the name of the gas being produced?

4. Find out the weight of a large loaf of bread. (All large loaves are the same weight; this is controlled by law.) Use this information to give a reason why the dough is divided into pieces weighing 860g.

5. The oven temperature is set at over 200°C, but the temperature at the middle of the loaf does not rise above 100°C. Give an explanation for this.

6. If the cooling system for the baked loaves was not working properly and the bread was being packed warm, describe what you might see inside the bread bag.

Understanding Industrial Practices: Food Technology © Nelson Thornes 2005

20 hygiene

Name ....

Form/group .... **Date** ....

1 Give three reasons why **hygiene** is important wherever food is being handled.

2 Look at the drawing below and circle every example you can see of poor hygiene. Then in the space below, explain what is wrong in the drawing.

3 Write instructions for **cleaning** a piece of kitchen equipment that you use, e.g. a food blender.

Further work

Visit the website at *www.good2eat.info* to pick up more hygiene information and test yourself on your knowledge.

Understanding Industrial Practices: Food Technology © Nelson Thornes 2005

21 industrial practices

Name ....

Form/group .... Date ....

1. You have been asked to design and manufacture a range of 'healthy option' chilled ready-meals, suitable for serving as in-flight meals for children. Think about the following questions:

   - What nutritional content is needed?

   - What **aesthetic** and sensory qualities are needed?

   - What food ingredients will be suitable for the **target market group**?

2. List the industrial designing and manufacturing activities that would be used in the production of in-flight meals for children.

Further work

Identify six industrial designing activities and six industrial manufacturing activities that you could use in your own coursework project.

Designing activities

Manufacturing activities

22

method of production (1)

Name ....

Form/group .... **Date** ....

1 Choose a food product that you have made by **one-off production**.

2 List the manufacturing processes you used to make it.

3 Give three reasons why you have made your product as a one-off production.

4 Describe three ways in which your **method of production** could be improved, or simplified, to make it more suitable for manufacturing your product in **high volume**. You need to think about how you could:

- use **standard components** wherever possible
- use different ingredients if necessary to reduce costs
- describe the equipment you would need to make the product efficiently
- alter or eliminate any **finishing processes** you have used
- control the **quality** to make sure each product is satisfactory.

23   method of production (2)

Name ....

Form/group .... **Date** ....

You have been asked to design a range of small decorated cakes suitable for a Halloween Party for teenagers.

1   Sketch ideas for decorating the cakes.

2   Choose a suitable **method of production** for your cakes. They must be quick and easy to manufacture. You need to think about:

- the scale of production, i.e. how many cakes you need to make
- how much time you have available to make the cakes in time for Halloween. You cannot make the cakes too soon before Halloween or they will go stale.
- what ingredients you need to order for delivery in time for you to make the cakes
- the **finishing processes** you will use and how skilled you are
- how, and where, in the manufacturing process you can use **quality control (QC)** checks and tests.

24 nutritional information

The data below comes from two different **brands** of canned baked beans in tomato sauce. Read the data and then answer the questions below.

Nutritional information (typical values per 100g):

	Brand A	Brand B
Energy	331kJ/78kcal	279kJ/66kcal
Protein	4.6g	4.6g
Carbohydrate (of which sugars)	16.6g 5.5g	11.3g 3.4g
Fat (of which saturates)	0.3g 0.1g	0.2g (trace)
Fibre	3.5g	3.7g
Sodium	0.5g	0.3g

1 Give two ways in which baked beans can make a useful nutritional contribution to the diet.

2 Which brand of baked beans includes people trying to control their weight in its **target market group**? Explain your answer.

3 What is the **Recommended Nutrient Intake (RNI)** for **protein** for someone of your age and sex? If you ate a 60g portion of baked beans how much protein would that provide? What proportion of your daily requirement is that?

4 Give two reasons why protein is important in our diet.

Further work

1 What is the **Estimated Average Requirement (EAR)** for energy for someone of your age and sex? Give a reason why you might need more energy than the EAR.

2 Calculate the nutritional content of a product you are making. Explain why it is suitable for someone in your target market group.

25   pastry

Pastry is a food material that can be made in the kitchen or factory, or it can be bought-in as a **standard component**. Bought-in components can save time or reduce the manufacturing skills needed.

Carry out work to decide what type of pastry is most useful for making mince pies.

You will need some pre-made shortcrust pastry, puff pastry and filo pastry. You will need to know the cost of each type of pastry.

1. The class divides into three groups.

2. One group of students make mince pies using shortcrust pastry, one group use puff pastry and one group use filo pastry.

3. Carry out sensory analysis on the mince pies to find out which type of pastry most people prefer. You can use a sensory evaluation method like the one in worksheet 43.

4. Work out the cost of a **batch** of pies using each type of pastry. Which pies will offer best value for money for a family?

Further work

Describe a product that you would choose to make using:

    a) shortcrust pastry

    b) puff pastry

    c) filo pastry.

Give a reason for your choice in each case.

26 product analysis (1)

Analysing a commercially-produced food product can help you understand how **product development teams** solve problems. Choose a food product such as a ready-meal or a pizza.

Using the key terms below to help you, describe the product's features.

1 List and describe three special features of the product.

2 List and describe two good points about the product.

3 List and describe two bad points about the product.

4 Using the information you have gained, explain why the **target market group** would buy the product.

KEY WORDS

Function
E.g. main meal; snack; treat: how well does it perform its function?

Nutritional content
E.g. good source of nutrients; high in salt; sugar; saturated fat.

Appearance
Good **aesthetic** qualities; attractive ingredients.

Preparation required
E.g. ready to eat; oven or microwave cooking required; preparation time.

Storage
E.g. chilled; frozen; stored in a cupboard.

Sensory quality
Taste; texture; colour.

Size and/or weight of product
E.g. number of helpings.

Target market group
Consumer group that the **manufacturer** aims to sell to.

Further work

Look at magazines and select a food product that is marketed for people who take part in a sporting activity.

- Investigate the properties of the ingredients used in the product.
- Research the nutritional needs of people undertaking the sporting activity.
- Draw up a table to show why the product makes a useful contribution to the nutritional needs of people who take part in sport.

Understanding Industrial Practices: Food Technology © Nelson Thornes 2005

27 product analysis (2)

The **manufacturer** of dried 'cuppa' soup mixes is a **secondary food** processor. The company buys in all its ingredients as **standard components**. These are mixed together and the correct weight of soup mix is packed into a sachet. Vegetable pieces such as diced carrots must be small. Their size is defined in the **specification** that the soup manufacturer agrees with the dried vegetable supplier.

What to do:
Investigate a dried soup mix and its **packaging**.

You will need:
- a packet containing sachets of dried vegetable soup
- a sachet of the dried soup mix
- a small bowl and a kettle for boiling water.

1. Open the sachet of soup and examine the contents. Identify pieces of each vegetable named on the ingredients list.

2. Take out one piece of carrot. Place it on a piece of paper and draw around it.

3. Put the piece of carrot into a small bowl and pour boiling water on to it. (**TAKE CARE** when using boiling water.) After 5 minutes remove the carrot with a spoon, dry it carefully and draw around it again.

   a) Describe the change in size of the carrot piece (e.g. half as large again; doubled in size). Explain the reason for the change in size.

   b) Why must the vegetable pieces in a 'cuppa' soup be small? Suggest how the dried vegetable supplier might remove any pieces of carrot that are too large for supplying to the soup manufacturer.

4. The packaging is made up of the sachet that contains the soup and the outer (the box the sachets are sold in). Explain how the manufacturer has used **colour** and design in the inner sachet and the outer packaging.

5. What **packaging material** is the outer made of? What advantages does this type of packaging material have for:

   a) the manufacturer

   b) the **consumer**

   c) the environment?

6. Many 'cuppa' soups are bought by working people to use at lunchtime. List the features of the product that you think make it attractive for this use.

28   Product Data Management

Name ....

Form/group... Date ....

1 Explain three key features of a **Product Data Management (PDM)** system.

2 Give four benefits of using a PDM system:

- for product development

- for manufacturing.

3 The use of **computer systems** enables **manufacturers** to source ingredients on a global scale.

   a) List four fresh vegetables in your local supermarket that have been imported from a country outside the EU, which can also be grown in the UK.

   b) What effect does growing vegetables for UK supermarkets have on the economy of a developing country such as Kenya?

29   product specification (1)

Manufacturers often use computer software to develop standard **specification** forms. This saves time and is more efficient because it allows all specifications to be written in the same way.

Design the format for a **product specification** form that you can use for different food products. The format needs to allow space for the following information:

- The name and description of the product.

- The recipe and processing details for the product.

- **Quality control (QC)** tests for the product, with **quality indicators** and their target values and **tolerances**.

- Nett weight of each product.

- Details of **packaging** to be used.

- Storage requirements for the product.

- **Shelf life** of the product.

Further work

1. Ask someone else to explain how to make your product using only the information you have given in the product specification.

2. Check the **quality** of your product against the targets and tolerances given in your product specification. This will help to ensure that you make a high quality product.

30   product specification (2)

The analysis of a successful food product can help your understanding of the importance of a **product specification**.

1. Examine either a low-cost or an expensive food product. Ask the following questions:

   - What makes the product successful? Is it the **brand** image; **packaging**; cost or ingredients?

   - Is the product well designed, so that it meets the needs of its **target market group**? Does it come in a range of pack sizes and different varieties?

   - Is the product value for money? How does it compare in price and **quality** with similar products?

   - How is the product made? Does it have many ingredients, or just a few?

   - What processes are used to make the product?

   - Is the product well made? Has it got a good **aesthetic** appeal? Is the packaging in good condition?

   - How long is the **shelf life**?

   - How is the product stored? Does it need chilled or frozen storage?

2. Record your answers then produce a product specification for the product.

   - Include a description of the product.

   - Remember to include details of the ingredients and processes used in making and packaging the product.

31   production line

Name ....

Form/group... **Date** ....

Products such as pizzas and ready-meals contain some ingredients that can be added by machine and some that must be weighed out and added by hand by workers on a **production line**. If you look at an uncooked product, such as the topping on a pizza, you can see what ingredients have been used and work out how it has been made.

You will need:
A factory-made pizza, e.g. ham and mushroom, pepperoni or vegetable feast.

1. In the space below, list the ingredients used for the pizza topping. (Don't cheat by looking at the **ingredients list** on the packaging!) As far as possible, list the ingredients in the order they have been placed on to the pizza.

2. Underline any ingredients you think might have been added by machine. Explain why machines are unsuitable for adding the other ingredients.

3. Construct a **flow chart** for the production of the pizza topping.

Further work

1. Describe the **size reduction** operations that have been used in preparing the ingredients for the topping.
2. Explain what is meant by the term '**tolerance**'.
3. Explain why tolerance is important for the weight of the vegetable ingredients in the topping.

32 production line simulation

Name ....

Form/group .... **Date** ....

Flow chart symbols

○   An operation is performed on the food material.

☐   An inspection (or test) is made on the food material.

▽   The food is stored.

D   Delay. The food is kept in one place for a period of time.

⇨   The food is transported from one place to another.

Try simulating a **production line** to manufacture sandwiches in **high volume**. You will need to work in a team of 4–6 people.

1. Your task is to design and manufacture sandwiches using bread as a **standard component** and a simple filling of grated cheese and sliced tomatoes.

2. Give your team a time limit during which you need to make as many high **quality** sandwiches as possible. Work as a team to plan your production.
   - Decide how much of each ingredient you will need for each sandwich.
   - List the different processes, materials and equipment you will need to use.
   - Using the symbols above, draw a **flow chart** showing the manufacturing processes you will use. Show where and how you will check the quality of your product.
   - Work out how long each operation will take. Share out the work with your team so that everyone has a fair share.
   - Manufacture the sandwiches with each team member doing one task. Check for quality as you go.
   - Run a final quality check and count how many satisfactory quality sandwiches you have made in the time available. Work out the percentage of sandwiches that are not of satisfactory quality.
   - Evaluate how each team member worked. Did anyone have too much/not enough to do?

Further work

Decide how you would package and store the sandwiches for sale, to ensure a good standard of **hygiene** for your **consumers**.

See worksheet 1: batch production for other ideas on how to set up a design and production team.

33 prototyping

Making a **prototype** is a key part of the **product development (PD)** process. It helps you try out a recipe idea early on, before you have spent a lot of time developing a product that no one may like, or that might be too expensive for anyone to buy.

In worksheet 11 you developed a **design specification** and recipes for a nutritious soup for elderly people.

1. Use one of your recipes to make some soup.

2. Decide what information you need to find out about your soup. Write out a simple questionnaire for **consumers** to complete.

3. Carry out **sensory analysis** on your soup. You could ask grandparents to taste it or try the soup out in a local community drop-in café.

   Important food safety note: Make sure that if you have to transport your soup it is kept chilled at all times.

4. Use **feedback** from the sensory analysis to help you decide if the soup meets the requirements of your **target market group**.

5. Carry out your own evaluation of the prototype soup. Use the following questions to guide you:
   - What problems did you have in getting the ingredients you needed?
   - Were there any problems with finding the equipment that you needed to make the soup?
   - How long did it take to make the soup? Could you reduce the time needed to make the soup?
   - How much would it cost the consumer for one portion of the soup?

6. Use feedback from your own experience in making the soup to decide if you need to make any modifications to the recipe.

7. Adapt the recipe as necessary in order to meet the design specification.

34   quality

Name ....

Form/group .... **Date** ....

1. In a team, compare two similar products, such as cornflakes, made by different **manufacturers**. One product should cost more than the other. You could compare a **brand** of cornflakes with a supermarket's **'own-label'** product. You will need to know the price for the same quantity of each product.

2. In the table below, write notes to compare the main **quality** features of each product. Give each product a score out of 10 for each feature (0 = very bad, 10 = brilliant).

	Product 1	Product 2
Appearance (e.g. look at colour and size of flakes to judge the aesthetic value)		
Quality of manufacture (e.g. look to see any variation in colour and any broken flakes at the bottom of the bag)		
Quality of the packaging (e.g. does the packaging tear easily? How has colour been used in the packaging design?)		
Nutritional value of the food (e.g. any differences in vitamins and minerals declared as present in the food)		
Sensory quality of the food. Prepare some cornflakes (follow any serving suggestion on the packet) then taste them.		

3. State which of the products is the more expensive and why it costs more.

4. Who do you think is the **target market group** for each product?

5. Explain how each product meets the requirements of its target market group.

6. Write a **manufacturing specification** for the higher priced product.

| **35** | **quality assurance** |

Name ....

Form/group .... **Date** ....

You will need to include **quality assurance (QA)** procedures when making your food products to ensure their high **quality**.

1 Explain the difference between QA and **quality control (QC)**.

2 Look at this manufacturing **flow chart** for spaghetti bolognese, chilled, ready-meals.

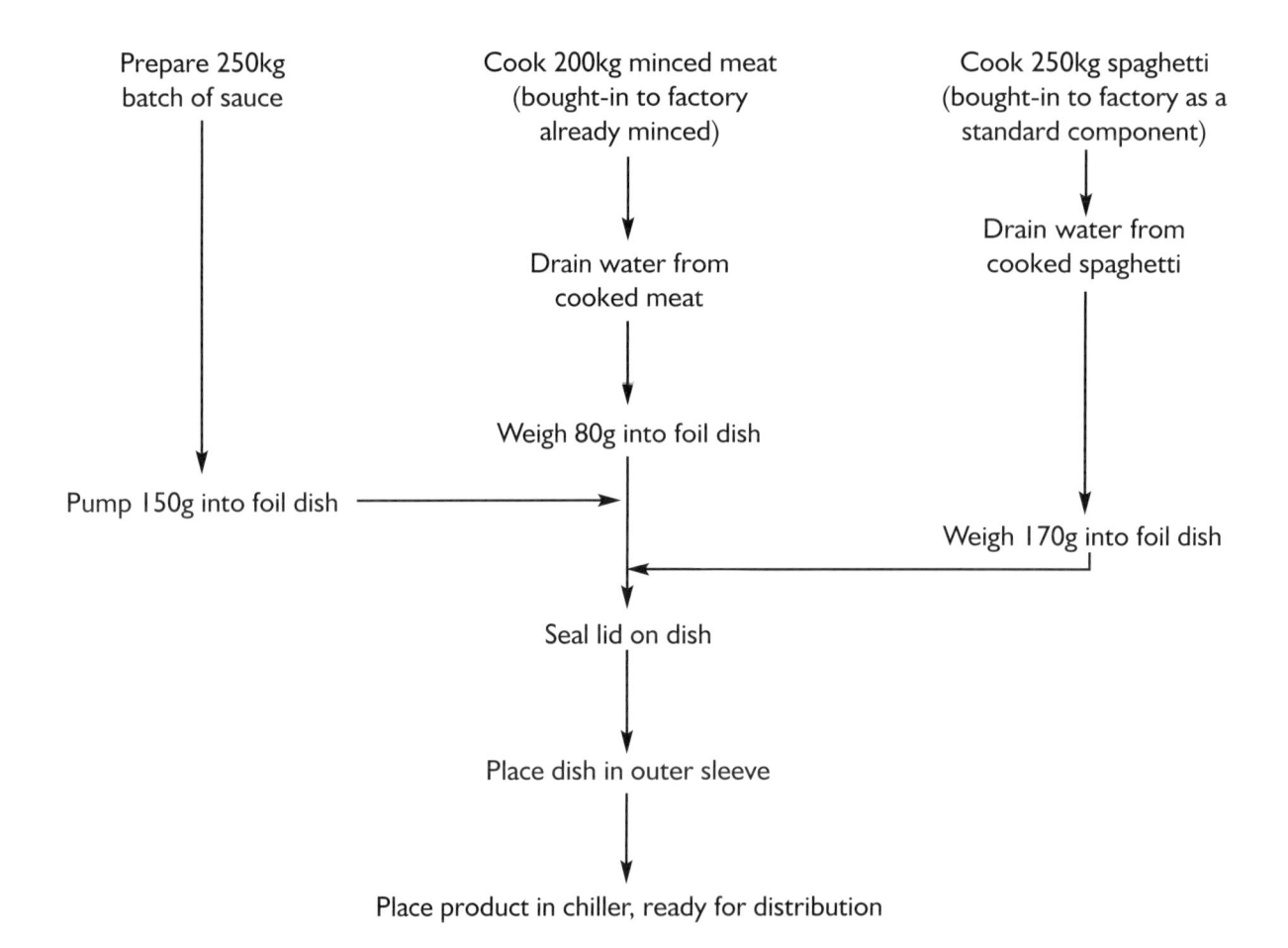

```
Prepare 250kg          Cook 200kg minced meat      Cook 250kg spaghetti
batch of sauce         (bought-in to factory       (bought-in to factory as a
                       already minced)             standard component)
     │                         │                           │
     │                         ▼                           ▼
     │                   Drain water from           Drain water from
     │                   cooked meat                cooked spaghetti
     │                         │                           │
     │                         ▼                           │
     │                   Weigh 80g into foil dish          │
     │                         │                           │
     ▼                         │                           ▼
Pump 150g into foil dish ─────►│◄──────────────── Weigh 170g into foil dish
                               ▼
                         Seal lid on dish
                               │
                               ▼
                         Place dish in outer sleeve
                               │
                               ▼
                    Place product in chiller, ready for distribution
```

3 Mark on the flow chart where you would carry out QC checks as part of a QA system to ensure the spaghetti bolognese is of a high quality.

4 Describe the QC checks you would carry out.

Further work

Draw a flow chart showing how your product is made to help you decide where to carry out QC checks.

36 quality control (1)

Name ....

Form/group .... **Date** ....

Analyse the **quality** of a commercially made, pre-packed pizza, using the quality checks in the table below. For each quality check, write a sentence or two to describe your findings.

Quality check	Result of the quality check
Check the outer packaging for damage	
Check the inner packaging for damage	
Check the pizza for damage to its base or for any topping which has come away from the pizza	
Check the aesthetic quality of the pizza	
Check that the weight of the pizza is not less than that given on the packaging	
Check that all ingredients given as part of the topping are present	
Follow the cooking instructions on the packaging. Check that the pizza is not overcooked or undercooked (you can use a temperature probe to check that the temperature in the centre is above 75°C).	
Check that the texture and taste of the pizza are satisfactory.	

Understanding Industrial Practices: Food Technology © Nelson Thornes 2005

37   quality control (2)

Name ....

Form/group... **Date** ....

1. Look at the **flow chart** on page 7 showing how canned rice pudding is manufactured.

2. Write down the stages where you think the **manufacturer** will have **quality control (QC)** checks and tests carried out to ensure that the rice pudding is always of a high **quality**.

3. Suggest suitable QC tests that could be carried out at the points you have identified.

Further work

For your next product, consider the quality tests and inspection processes that you will need to carry out.

Using the symbols below, draw a flow chart to show where and how your quality checks will take place. Include any **feedback** loops to show how feedback is incorporated into your **quality system**. Describe any changes you make to the design, manufacturing processes, production or **finishing processes** of your food product to ensure that it will be of a high quality.

Flow chart symbols

◯   An operation is performed on the food material.

▢   An inspection (or test) is made on the food material.

▽   The food is stored.

D   Delay. The food is kept in one place for a period of time.

⇨   The food is transported from one place to another.

38   quality indicators

Name ....

Form/group .... Date ....

1. Examine the biscuits in a packet of plain biscuits. **Texture** and diameter (if the biscuits are round) or length and width (if the biscuits are rectangular) are examples of **quality indicators** that the **manufacturer** has used.

2. Decide which terms best describe the texture of the biscuits. Here are some words that might be useful; you can think of others as well.

   - Hard
   - Soft
   - Crunchy
   - Chewy
   - Gritty
   - Dry
   - Moist

3. Suggest how the texture of the biscuits might be described in the **product specification**. Include **tolerances** in your description.

4. Are all the biscuits in the packet the same size? What problems do you think it could cause the manufacturer if there was a lot of variation between biscuits?

5. Suggest two more quality indicators that the manufacturer has used to check the **quality** of the biscuits.

6. Explain what is meant by the terms 'attribute' and 'variable' for quality indicators. State whether texture, diameter and the two quality indicators you have suggested are attributes or variables.

Further work

List the quality indicators for a product you have made. Explain the **quality control (QC)** checks you used to ensure that your product conformed to its product specification.

39 quality of design

Name ....

Form/group... Date ....

1 Explain what is meant by **quality of design**.

2 Describe the difference between quality of design and **quality of manufacture**.

3 You have been given a **design brief** to design and develop a fruit 'smoothie' made with summer fruits, with 10–25 year olds as the **target market group**.

Describe the steps you would take to evaluate your **prototype** smoothie to ensure that you have achieved good quality of design.

You should consider the following questions:

- Do members of your target market group like the product?
- What size packs should it be sold in?
- Are the ingredients readily available?
- Can the product be made and marketed at a suitable price?
- Can the product be manufactured in sufficient quantity to satisfy demand?
- Can it be sold in outlets that will be used by the target market group?

40   quality of manufacture

You should always aim to manufacture a high **quality** product that meets your **specifications** and the needs of your **target market group**.

1. Write a **product specification** and a **manufacturing process specification** for your next food product.

2. Produce a **flow chart** to show the order of the processes you will use.

   a) Show where you will carry out **quality control (QC)** checks in your manufacturing process.

   b) List and explain the **quality indicators** you will use, showing how you will check for quality.

3. Evaluate your food product by comparing it with your specifications.

4. Obtain **feedback** about your product from your target market group.

5. Using feedback information, explain how the **quality of manufacture** of your product could be improved.

41 risk assessment

Name ....

Form/group... Date ....

1 Look at the **flow chart** showing commercial crisp manufacture on page 76.

2 Describe one **hazard** associated with the production of crisps that could cause a risk to the **health and safety (H&S)** of:

   a) the workers in the factory

   b) the **consumer**

   c) the environment.

   In each case, state the risk that is associated with the hazard.

3 For each risk that you have identified, list the steps that the **manufacturer** should take to minimise the risk of something going wrong.

Further work

1 Draw a flow chart for the next product you are going to make. Identify the hazards and risks associated with making your product.

2 Write a list of safety rules to follow that will ensure any risks are minimised.

42   scaling-up

Name ....

Form/group .... Date ....

Use a recipe for a Victoria sponge to **scale-up** for **high-volume production**.

1. In the third column in the table below, list differences at each stage of manufacture in **one-off** and high volume production.

One-off production	High-volume production	Differences
Ingredients stored in fridge and cupboard	Flour in bulk storage tank; liquid egg in chilled tank; sugar in large bags; fat in chiller	
Weigh ingredients; blend together as all-in-one mix using kitchen mixer	Meter flour and egg into mixer, add weighed fat, sugar and water. Computer-aided manufacture (CAM) mixes the ingredients and pumps the mixture to a production line.	
Mix is spooned evenly into two cake-baking tins	Computer controlled amount of cake mixture is deposited into several tins simultaneously **Point A**	
Sponge baked in oven	Sponges baked as tins on conveyor travel through a tunnel oven	
Cooked cake removed from tin by hand, cooled, jam added to one half with a spoon, two halves put together	Cooked cakes removed from tins by hand, cooled, jam added to one half by machine, two halves put together	
Sponge ready for eating	Sponges packed into boxes, sealed, and date coded by machine, passed through metal detector and bulk packed into large boxes for distribution	

2. Write in the weights below of ingredients needed for one-off production, then work out the weights needed to make 50kg of sponge mixture.

Ingredient	One-off	High volume 50kg mix
Flour	g	kg
Sugar	g	kg
Fat	g	kg
Egg	g	kg
Baking powder	g	kg

3. Which production method results in a greater amount of waste mixture that does not get made into sponges? Explain your answer. What effect does reducing waste have on production costs?

4. Describe a **quality control (QC)** check that could be carried out at **Point A**.

Understanding Industrial Practices: Food Technology © Nelson Thornes 2005

43 sensory analysis

A fresh fruit salad is a refreshing dessert. Fruits that are included in the salad will add **colour** and **texture** as well as **taste**.

What to do:

Investigate the use of different fruits based on their **aesthetic** properties and the eating **quality** requirements of a fruit salad.

You will need:

Apple juice and lemon juice and as many different fruits as possible from the following two lists:
- List a): Banana; apple; pear; different coloured melons; pineapple; green grapes; grapefruit.
- List b): Peach; orange; kiwi fruit; green grapes; black grapes; plum; cherries; strawberries.

You will need to work in three teams:

Team 1 can use only fruits from list a).

Team 2 can use only fruits from list b).

Team 3 can use two fruits from list a) and three fruits from list b).

1. In your team, choose five fruits for your fruit salad and decide how much of each fruit to use.

2. Prepare your fruit by peeling/cutting/slicing/removing stones or pips as needed and place it in a bowl.

3. Add apple juice and 5–10cm³ of lemon juice to the bowl. Gently stir the fruit in the juice until all the fruit is coated.

4. Prepare a **sensory analysis** table to give to student members of a **taste** panel. You could adapt the table on page 73. You could also ask your panellists, 'Why do you like fruit salad X (or Y or Z) the best?' This will help you to decide which is the most important aesthetic quality for your **consumers**.

5. Ask as many students as possible to taste the fruit salads and give them a score.

6. Count up the scores for each salad. The one with the highest score is the most popular.
   - Which fruit salad was the most popular?
   - What was the main reason given for choosing a favourite (e.g. colour, size of fruit pieces, liked those particular fruits).

7. Evaluate all the information you have collected and develop a recipe for a fruit salad that you think will appeal to most students.

Further work

If you have a school canteen, ask if your fruit salad can be added to the menu.

44 systems

Name ....

Form/group .... **Date** ....

Computer controlled mixers enable the rapid production of batter for cake production. To make this **system** work there must be three pieces of hardware: a mixer; a computer with a control panel; and a method for programming the recipe into the computer.

This system is represented by the block diagram below.

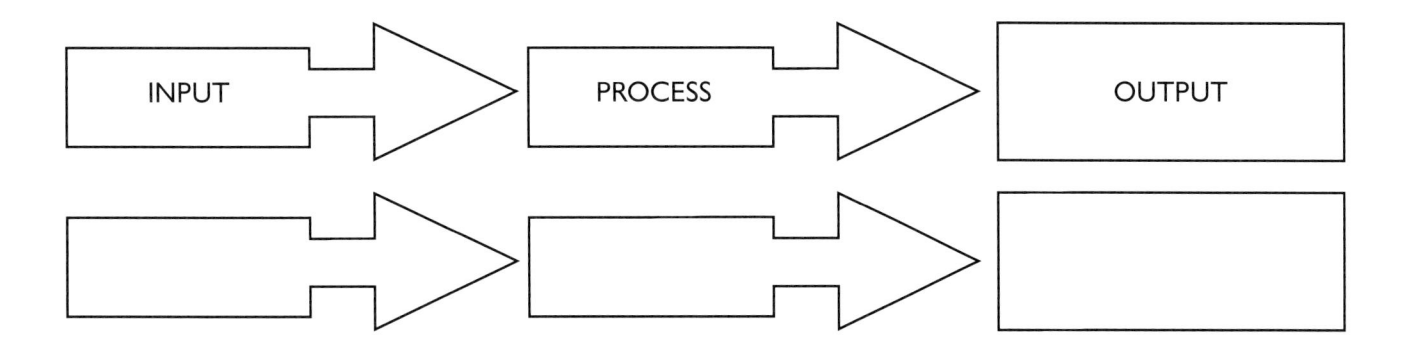

| INPUT | ⇒ | PROCESS | ⇒ | OUTPUT |

| | ⇒ | | ⇒ | |

1 Put the correct piece of hardware in the correct place in the block diagram.

2 Name the kind of system represented in the block diagram.

3 Using a new block diagram, explain how you could improve this system.

Understanding Industrial Practices: Food Technology © Nelson Thornes 2005

45 using a systems approach (1)

You can plan a project using a **systems** approach. This can help you to plan your work better and enable you to use **feedback** to monitor the **quality** of your product.

1. Make a list of the ingredients, **standard components**, tools and equipment you used to make your last product. Include all the activities and processes you used. For example, you could include all the research, designing, manufacturing and evaluation activities. Remember to include all the processes you used in preparing your ingredients and making your product. Remember to list all your product 'output', such as pasta and a sauce.

2. Draw up a table with three columns headed Input, Process and Output. You could use a table similar to the one below. Fill in the columns with the appropriate **raw materials**, standard components, activities, processes and product output from your list.

Input	Process	Output

3. Using your Input, Process and Output lists, design a simple open loop system using a block diagram template similar to the one used in worksheet 44.

4. Using a block diagram template similar to the one shown below, organise your Input and Process lists into two separate vertical **flow charts**. In each flow chart show the sequence of the activities and processes you undertook to make your product. By doing this you will have created sub-systems within your large system. Remember to write your product Output in the output box.

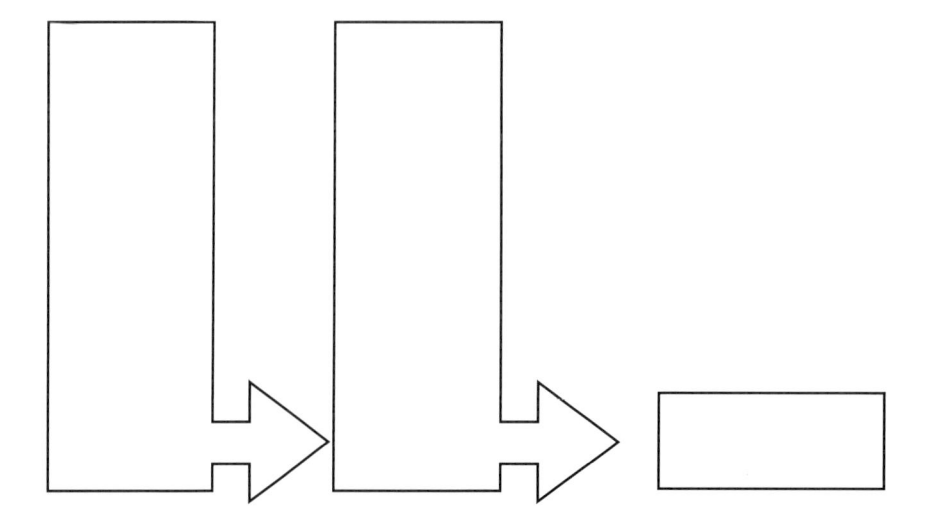

46 using a systems approach (2)

You can plan a project using a **systems** approach. This can help you to plan your work better and enable you to use **feedback** to monitor the **quality** of your product.

1 Undertake tasks 1–4 in worksheet 45.

2 You are now ready to introduce some quality checks into your system. Choose some, or all, of the following to test or check the quality of your product:

- Test **raw materials** and equipment.
- Check your product against your **design specification**.
- Check that all the ingredients have been weighed correctly.
- Check cooking temperatures and times.
- Check your product against your **product specification** and **manufacturing process specification**.
- Check that the product is stored correctly.
- Check that any instructions for use are suitable.

All of the tests or checks you have chosen can provide feedback to your quality system.

3 Using a block diagram template similar to the one shown below (and the information from your sub-systems block diagram produced in task 4 on worksheet 45), produce a new sub-systems diagram that includes feedback loops on the two sub-systems **flow charts**. This will show how quality checks can help monitor the quality of your product. By doing this you will have incorporated feedback into your system.

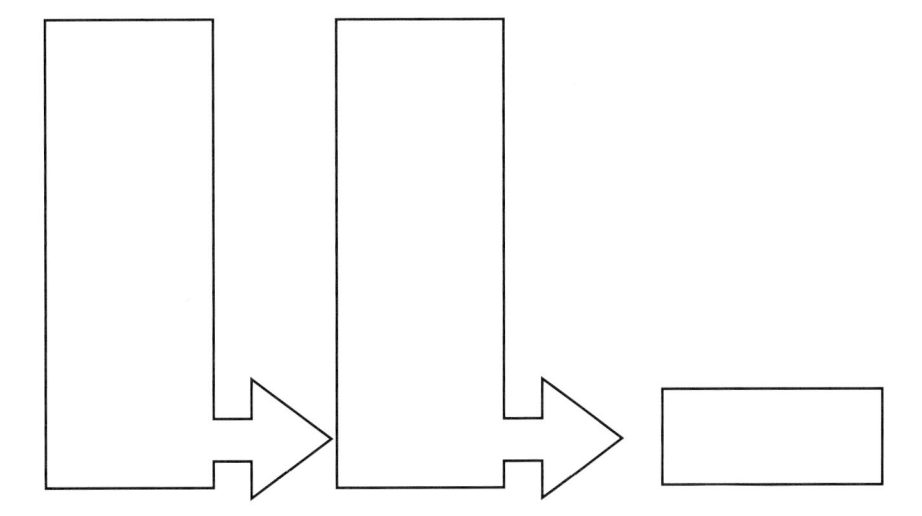

Further work

If you plan your next project using a systems approach you will be working in a similar way to industry. You will also help yourself to work more efficiently and to produce a high quality food product.

Understanding Industrial Practices: Food Technology © Nelson Thornes 2005

47   target market group

Name ....

Form/group .... Date ....

Some foods sold to **consumers** can be manufactured in more than one way. These different manufacturing methods often match the needs of different **target market groups**.

Investigate a soup that has been manufactured as:

    a) a fresh product, available in the chiller cabinet

    b) a canned product

    c) a dried soup mix.

You will need to know the price of each product.

Your soups should all be the same variety, e.g. cream of tomato or carrot and coriander. You will need pans and bowls, etc. for preparing the soups.

1   Before you open the soups, answer the following questions:

	Fresh soup	Canned soup	Dried soup
How many servings can be made from the pack?			
What is the cost per serving?			
How long does the soup take to prepare?			
Can any unused soup be kept and used later?			
Are there any special storage instructions?			
How long is the shelf life?			

2   Now prepare each soup according to the instructions given on the pack and taste it.

- Which soup did you like best? Give a reason for your answer.

- Which soup did you like least? Give a reason for your answer.

3   Make a list of the consumers you think most likely to buy each soup, e.g. working mums with a family to feed, or young couples having a dinner party. In each case, explain how you think the soup matches the needs of the target market group.

Further work

Imagine you are chef working in a canteen providing lunches and snacks for students.

- Make a list of food likes and dislikes for the students in your target market group.

- Use your lists of students' food likes and dislikes to design and make a fresh soup that will meet the requirements of your target market group.

48   testing

Name ....

Form/group .... **Date** ....

1. List the **stages of production** where a **manufacturer** would arrange to have tests carried out to make sure that products always meet their **product specification**.

2. Explain why it is important that tests on food ingredients and products are carried out in the same way, every time.

3. Tests can be carried out using **quality indicators** that are either attributes or variables. Suggest two attributes and two variables that might be used in **testing** a cheese and tomato sandwich.

4. Devise a test that could be carried out to make sure that a chicken nugget contains the correct ratio of coating to chicken. Write out a test method for your test.

49 values issues

Values issues have an important influence on our lives and on the products we use. Product developers and **manufacturers** have to carefully consider the values, needs and wants of the **target market group** at which the product is aimed.

You will need to make good use of social, cultural and environmental influences when you develop your own product ideas. It will help you to think about values issues if you ask some of the following questions when you undertake **product analysis**.

About the product
- What is the target market group for this product? Does this group have any special needs, e.g. vegetarian; low fat; organic?
- What makes this product attractive to the target market group?
- Would you like to buy and eat this product? Why?

About the need for the product
- Is the product a basic food, a snack or a 'treat'?
- How well does the product meet the needs of the target market group?
- Who benefits from the manufacture of the product? How will they benefit?

The design of the product
- Is it a **branded** product? How is it special?
- What kind of image does the product provide?
- Is there a choice of **flavours** and product sizes available?
- What kind of values influenced the design of the product? Cultural, social or environmental?

The product manufacture
- What ingredients and processes are used to make the product? Why?
- Where do the ingredients come from? Is sustainability an issue?
- What impact does supplying these ingredients have upon the people and the environment that supplies them?
- What happens to any waste produced during manufacture?
- What skills are needed to make the product?
- Where is the product made?

Marketing and advertising the product
- How is the product advertised?
- How and where is the product sold?
- Is the product sold at a suitable cost for the target market group?
- How does the price compare with other similar products?

Use and disposal of the product
- What energy will be needed in the preparation of the food for eating?
- Can the **packaging** be recycled? Who pays the cost of recycling?

Further work

Research the work of the Fair Trade organisation in helping developing countries to produce and market food.